Be inspired! To Suzanne
To God be the ♡ laurie
Glory! 3/14/24

SO-BAY-594

RELOAD LOVE

LENYA HEITZIG

HARVEST HOUSE PUBLISHERS
EUGENE, OREGON

Cover by Jason Gabbert Design

Cover photos © Petr Bonek, siraphat, Ekaterina Zimodro, Photo Boutique, donatas1205 / Shutterstock

Backcover Author Photo by Matt and Tish Photography

Published in association with William K. Jensen Literary Agency, 119 Bampton Court, Eugene, Oregon 97404.

Reload Love

Copyright © 2018 Lenya Heitzig
Published by Harvest House Publishers
Eugene, Oregon 97408
www.harvesthousepublishers.com

ISBN 978-0-7369-7035-8 (pbk.)
ISBN 978-0-7369-7036-5 (eBook)

Library of Congress Cataloging-in-Publication Data
Names: Heitzig, Lenya, author.
Title: Reload Love / Lenya Heitzig.
Description: Eugene, Oregon : Harvest House Publishers, 2018.
Identifiers: LCCN 2018000690 (print) | LCCN 2018018070 (ebook) | ISBN
    9780736970365 (ebook) | ISBN 9780736970358 (pbk.)
Subjects: LCSH: Church work with children. | Missions. | Reload Love
    (Organization) | Heitzig, Lenya.
Classification: LCC BV2616 (ebook) | LCC BV2616 .H45 2018 (print) | DDC
    267/.13--dc23
LC record available at https://lccn.loc.gov/2018000690

Printed in the United States of America

18 19 20 21 22 23 24 25 26 / BP-SK / 10 9 8 7 6 5 4 3 2 1

Contents

To Aram, the eight-year-old boy, who escaped the brutal attacks of ISIS on Mount Sinjar. Despite losing several family members, he found hope and healing on a playground built by Reload Love. It is for him and millions like him that we bring beauty from bullets.

O Lord, you hear the desire of the afflicted;
you will strengthen their heart;
you will incline your ear
to do justice to the fatherless and the oppressed,
so that man who is of the earth
may strike terror no more.

PSALM 10:17-18 ESV

With Gratitude...

To my husband, Skip Heitzig, thank you for marrying me and embarking on the journey of a lifetime where God turned a little home Bible study into a megachurch with eternal impact. You embraced the vision God gave me to impact children caught in the crossfire of terrorism. Because you opened your heart and great doors of opportunity, Reload Love has armed children with hope across the globe. Team Heitzig for life!

To Franklin Graham, president of Samaritan's Purse International, I will always be grateful for your gutsy approach to reaching "the least of these" with the gospel of Jesus Christ and encouraging me to do the same. Skip and I have been privileged to join you where devastation hits— whether the killing fields of Rwanda, the frontlines of the conflict in Iraq, or the battered shores of Japan post-tsunami. Can't stop, won't stop!

To Dave Eubank, director of Free Burma Rangers, thank you for taking Malibu Barbie and teaching her how to be GI Jane. Your maxim to never make a decision based on fear, comfort, or pride challenges me to the core. Your example gave me courage to run through the jungle, crawl through ISIS tunnels, and summit Mount Sinjar to place playgrounds on top of battlegrounds. Never surrender!

Turning Battlegrounds into Playgrounds

I n 2015, streams of Yazidi refugees, escaping the atrocities of ISIS in the Sinjar region, found their way to a place called Khanke Camp, a sea of white tents provided by UNRCH, a United Nations' organization. All around them in the Kurdish wilderness, unseen and uncharted, were live land mines and discarded IEDs (improvised explosive devices) left behind by ISIS from when they had fled from advancing coalition forces. These fields, stretching for miles all the way to the mountains, were not places where anyone could simply wander around. Children could not run through the tall grass. Certain areas had been cleared, but the camp was an island in the middle of an abandoned battlefield.

It was early in the long and winding journey of Reload Love, and my husband, Skip, scouted out potential partners for us in the middle of those windswept plains of Kurdistan. We were a young organization still trying to figure out how to help children impacted by terror, and we wanted to team up with others already doing that kind of work in the region. Providing playgrounds had just begun pinging our radar as a possible way of alleviating the pain and trauma inflicted on children by terrorism.

Skip was shown around Khanke Camp. He saw one-room tents housing families, some of which held more than ten people. Four tents shared one toilet, and there were eight tents for every one shower. Do the math—that's more than 40 people sharing one toilet, more than 80 people sharing one shower. Eventually the camp would house 45,000 people inside those barbed-wire fences, while another 20,000 squatters surrounded the perimeter, looking for safety, food, and shelter. That's 65,000 people, practically the population of a city, and every single one of them was displaced. No employment. Barely enough food and water. And for the time being, nowhere to go.

As Skip was led through the community, he passed a group of kids and noticed they were in the midst of an elaborate game of make-believe. Their play reminded him of his childhood in Apple Valley, California, the home of western movie stars Roy Rogers and Dale Evans. Skip and his brother had often reenacted the Wild West, with one of them impersonating the sheriff and the other wearing a black cowboy hat, taking on the role of the bad guy. They had spent many afternoons like that, chasing each other around the backyard, wielding their pretend six-shooters, facing each other in duels.

"Ohhh," Skip and his brother had groaned, collapsing to the dirt in mock agony, clutching their gut. "You got me."

"What are those boys doing?" Skip asked the interpreter, intrigued by the children's game.

"They're playing," the interpreter said.

"I can see that. But what are they playing? Can you ask them?"

The young Kurdish volunteer called the kids over. They approached, laughing and chatting, each one pushing to the front of the group, simultaneously excited and bashful to speak to the tall, white American. After a rapid-fire, back-and-forth conversation, the boys ran off and continued their game in the narrow alleys between the long rows of white tents. In moments, they disappeared, but Skip could still hear their shouts. The interpreter turned to give Skip the explanation.

"They told me they are playing war. They are fighting each other. Some of the boys are the Iraqi army or Peshmerga, and the other boys are pretending to be ISIS."

Children will always play with what they're given, won't they? They will create their own toys if they don't have any. Cardboard boxes, sticks, rocks: A child's imagination can take anything and use it. In the Khanke Camp, the black cowboy hats of Skip's childhood were replaced with black ISIS flags. Killing was the game the children knew, and it was the game they played.

They were pretending to be ISIS, the very group that had displaced them.

Because they had nothing else.

We see images these days on our screens or in our newspapers, and when the images are too painful or horrific or sad, most of us turn away or change the channel. Few of us look at these images for more than two or three seconds. It's too awkward, too uncomfortable, too jarring. They hurt too much, and we are left with a feeling of helplessness, something we don't know what to do with. So we look away.

We've become used to averting our gaze. In essence, we've become blind. I think of one particular blind man's interaction with Jesus.

> So Jesus answered and said to him, "What do you want Me to do for you?" The blind man said to Him, "Rabboni, that I may receive my sight." Then Jesus said to him, "Go your way; your faith has made you well." And immediately *he received his sight and followed Jesus* on the road (Mark 10:51-52, emphasis added).

What can we do to be healed of this self-inflicted blindness?

Even if we see the images on television and don't look away, it's not on the screen for more than a flash. We're fed bite-size portions, only enough to keep us on the hook through the next commercial break. They tell us a body washed up on a beach or children were found in the rubble, but we don't actually see death—we are shown the outside of the ambulance or the waves on the sand or the workers combing the shore for clues. We look, we glance, but we don't see.

The horror is edited away.

Or is it?

Because no matter how the content is edited in the newsroom, no matter how quickly we avert our gaze, the horror remains. The little boy is dead and washed up on the shore—the reality of this does not change just because we look away. The child was in a building hit by a bomb and his mother is dead—changing our focus to something else doesn't keep it from being so. The little girl hid for days from ISIS, all alone—averting our gaze doesn't erase that experience from her memory.

We can look away and pretend that makes it all go away, but the horror is still very real.

We so rarely sit and look at an image long enough for it to evoke an emotion in us. We want to avoid the pain, but what we need is to sit and look at these images, give them the time they require to bring our emotions to the surface. This is a kind of pain we should allow ourselves to feel.

What do you want me to do for you?

Rabboni, that I may receive my sight.

I used to look away. I used to see the pain and avert my gaze. But not anymore. Now when I see a difficult image of a child impacted by terror, I take it in. I allow myself to feel the emotions. I often cry, or sit in breathless sadness, or grit my teeth in anger. When I allow myself to do that, it does a work in me that is hard to explain.

In letting myself feel, in allowing these emotions to rise, I arrive at another decision point—fight or flight? Will I let my emotions lead me into a place where I can fight the evil that caused this terror, or will I let my emotions drive me away into helplessness or despair?

I think of the firemen who ran toward the Twin Towers on 9/11. I think of my friends in Iraq who, day after day, work with children impacted by terror. I think of the good Samaritan and how, even after the religious people averted their gaze and crossed to the other side of the road, he did not. I think about my friend Dave Eubank, his family, and his Free Burma Ranger teams running toward the bullets. They see the same photos we see, but instead of looking the other way, they say, "Somebody needs to do something about that."

And they do something about it.

I have become one of these people. I can no longer sit on the sidelines looking only at the things that make me feel good. I have taken these images in, digested them, and now I have to do something.

What do you want me to do for you?

Rabboni, that I may receive my sight.

Not too long ago I read an article telling the story of how 110 refugees set out to cross the Mediterranean, attempting to make it from Libya to Italy. Imagine being crammed into a boat that holds twice as many people as it should. Imagine setting out to sea with a life vest that might be fake (smugglers have been known to provide inexpensive knock-offs). Imagine the tossing waves, the salt water spraying over you, the sound of people praying for their lives. Imagine children crying, screaming, asking for food or something to drink.

Imagine how it feels when water pools around your feet. Imagine the fear when the boat starts going down.

Of those 110 refugees who set out from Libya on that particular boat, 106 drowned after their craft sank in the Mediterranean Sea. Only four survivors were pulled from the water.

Many of these victims were children.

Lord, help us.

Two thousand sixteen was the deadliest year on record when it came to refugees fleeing over the water, with more than 5,000 deaths happening on journeys to Europe. Some people drowned. Some people were crushed during the passage, while others suffocated in the bellies of overcrowded boats.

If you've seen the photos, if you've really looked at them, you'll notice vessels full of beautiful African and Middle Eastern faces. The adults are anxious. Some of the children are crying and holding their heads in their hands while others stare solemnly ahead. In one picture I saw a toddler, too small for a life jacket, wearing pink-and-white-striped pajamas, screaming as she was lifted in a harness out of the boat and into a neighboring vessel. Three people huddled around her—her brother? Her mother? Her father?—trying to make sure her ride through the air was a gentle one. I'm sure they were telling her not to cry. I'm sure they were reassuring her they'd be with her in no time at all.

"Everything will be okay," I imagine them saying to her. "We're being rescued. It's okay."

Remember the photo of the Syrian boy sitting in the back of the ambulance, the boy pulled from the rubble after yet another airstrike? He waits there in stunned silence. He doesn't cry or scream or shout for his parents. His eyes are devoid of any emotion. His thick, dark hair is pointing here and there, the way a little boy's hair will sometimes look when he first wakes up. He is completely covered in a fine, gray dust so that he looks like a statue, and streaks of darker ash line his cheek, his forehead. The entire left side of his face is covered in slick, red blood. There is the shape of an animal on his shirt—a dragon? A bird? It's hard to tell. The dirt and dust and ash are too much to see through.

He looks like the shell of a human being, and he has not yet heard the news that one of his loved ones has died.

I know everyone around him—the doctors, the nurses, the ambulance drivers—was doing their job, doing what needed to be done, but when I see him sitting there by himself, his loneliness makes me weep. I want to go into that picture and pick him up, cradle him in my arms, and rock him. I want to sing to him. In that moment, right then, right there, it seems like everything childlike is sliding out of him—his innocence, his youth, his emotions. It's all evaporating. I have this crazy thought that if I pick him up and rock him, it will stop. I can somehow refill him with innocence. Everything would be okay if I could only hold him in my arms and look into his eyes.

What will we do in the face of these atrocities? Will we become uncomfortable and look away? Will we try to forget all the things we've seen? Or will we see, really see, and then let our emotions lead us into a new way of living?

There was the photo of the three-year-old Syrian boy lying limp on a Turkish beach. His family had been on the move for many years, in and out of Syria, trying to avoid war and terror and join other family members in Canada. On that particular night, they were desperate to get to the Greek island of Kos. That's when their overcrowded boat capsized. The little boy's body washed up on the sand the next morning, and in the photograph, he lies facedown, the shallow waves washing up around him. He wore a red T-shirt, navy-blue shorts, and small shoes, looking like any American toddler ready to go to the mall or preschool or the playground. He had dark hair and dark eyes. He looked like a boy pretending on the beach, getting ready to roll over or stand up and then run to his parents, laughing.

But he was dead.

The photo of him breaks my heart every time I see it.

Yet those who survive these perilous water crossings or incredible wilderness treks have further hurdles to face, even after they arrive at their destination. There are stories of refugees being stuck at border crossings or railroads or airports, in countries not willing to let them in. In many cases, no one wants them. No one. Where will they go? What kind of life will they live? What kind of work will they be able to do? What kind of education will they receive? So many of them have been running because of ISIS or other terror groups. Terror is destabilizing the world, and innocent people flee, looking for a better life.

As I watched these events play out on the world stage during the last ten years, as I stopped averting my gaze and let myself see what was going on, my heart was broken by questions that kept coming up repeatedly:

With millions and millions of people on the run, who is looking out for the children?

What can I do to help children impacted by terror?

I went to God and begged Him to let me help. If there was anything I could do, I wanted to do it. *What is this all about, God? Why have You put this on my heart, a nobody living in Albuquerque, New Mexico? Where is my mission field? Where are the children who need help and what can I do to help them?*

God gave me an answer, a very clear answer:

Terror is the enemy. Your mission field is anywhere that children are being impacted by terror.

So what do I do?

The answer was far simpler than I expected, the kind of answer that at first sounded powerless in the face of such overwhelming evil. But the answer I received was to love. It might sound idealistic or naïve or pie-in-the-sky, but this is God's answer to the greatest problem faced by mankind. Love. Love brought Jesus from heaven to earth. Love is both the motivating factor and the first action—it is the why and the how.

Love eventually took me to children in the farthest reaches of the world.

How can any of us watch the news, see the hate in the world, and respond with anything but love?

One year after Skip was in the Khanke Camp in Kurdistan, one year after he watched little boys pretending to be ISIS fighters, I went to that camp to see a playground we had built with the help and support of another wonderful NGO. Our team entered the overflowing camp through a heavily guarded checkpoint, and our hosts showed us the same never-ending sea of white tents. Very few of the people had been able to move on. Their life was there, in the camp, and there were few options for them.

The playground we had helped build during the previous year immediately stuck out, a primary-colored structure in the midst of an otherwise colorless environment. I walked around it, taking it all in. Children hung from every bar, swooped down the slides, and laughed with delight as the swings flew up and down. These were dozens of children whose play had shifted from pretending to be knife- or gun-wielding terrorists to the childish kind of play I remembered from when I was young.

Spin away your troubles.

Climb higher.

Soar above it all.

"Can we talk to the children?" I asked our hosts, and they said we could. I spotted a boy with a huge cropping of curly hair making his way across the monkey bars. His contagious grin spread from ear to ear.

"Hello!" I said to him, smiling. "What's your name?"

"My name is Aram," he said, almost laughing with happiness. "I'm in the second grade."

At that moment, his teacher was collecting the children to take them inside. She said we could come into the classroom if we wanted to talk a little longer with Aram, so we followed the crowd of chattering children into a bright, colorful room full of pint-size chairs and tables. It all felt so inviting. We sat at the front of the room below the chalkboard, adults in tiny chairs. Aram and his interpreter faced us.

Our cameraman, Nick, set up the angle as Jolene, our field assistant, did the interview.

"Do you like it here?"

"Yes, a lot," Aram said, the smile never leaving his face.

"That's great. What do you learn here?"

"We learn the alphabet and mathematics, but I like English the most." Aram smiled wider at that proclamation.

Jolene transitioned the conversation from the present to the past.

"Where are you from?"

"Sinjar."

My heart sank. I knew Sinjar.[1] The Sinjar Massacre took place on August 3, 2014, and had been one of the primary events that began drawing my heart to the Middle East. On that day 10,000 Yazidis were killed or enslaved. It was a genocidal attack by ISIS that started at two in the morning. It only took a few hours for ISIS to gain control of the Sinjar district, where 350,000 Yazidis lived. They were told to convert to Islam or die. Most would not convert. Those who escaped fled up Mount Sinjar and spent the ensuing weeks and months battling not only ISIS but starvation and exposure as well.

Of those who were captured, the men and women were separated. The men and older women were killed and dumped into mass graves. The younger women were taken to Mosul, and from there they were distributed throughout the ISIS "caliphate" to be raped or tortured or otherwise used as needed.

When Aram said he was from Sinjar, I could only imagine what his beautiful brown eyes had seen. I almost had to turn away, but I didn't. I was learning not to avert my gaze. I was learning to look, and to see.

"How did you get here?" Nick asked quietly.

Aram looked away for a moment, down at the floor, and his smile faded. When he spoke again it was in a quiet, gentle voice. "We were attacked by a group of people. The same group attacked my sister's house. These people were called Daesh."

Daesh is the Arabic name for ISIS.

Later we would learn that Aram had lost a family member along the journey.

"Do you feel safe here?"

"Yes," he said, his smile returning. "It is safe."

I will never forget Aram. I will never forget the first glimpse I had of the playground in Khanke Camp, the vibrant colors against the backdrop of white tents. I will never forget the way the Kurdish countryside stretched on in every direction, uninterrupted except by the invisible land mines and IEDs yet to be found.

By the time I met Aram, Reload Love had been in operation for a year. Meeting him caused things in my heart to break loose—I knew I definitely wanted to help children impacted by terror, and seeing him on the playground made me wonder if building those playgrounds was the way forward for us as an organization. On the one hand, it sounded too simple—how would building playgrounds help when there are so many other pressing needs? But I had seen firsthand how these safe spaces united people, gave children a place to recover, and could become a tool for churches to reach out to their neighbors.

I also knew in my heart that I wanted to step foot on Mount Sinjar. This was not a new goal, but talking with Aram made me feel even more determined. I wanted to go into the city of Sinjar and walk the streets, to bear witness to the atrocities that had taken place there. I wanted—as an American Christian woman—to be able to go to a place where the black flags of ISIS had once flown, held high by men who hated me, hated Christians, hated Muslims who disagreed with them, hated small children like Aram because they were Yazidi. I hoped someday to witness an end to the evil they had brought to that city.

This is the story of my journey to Sinjar. This is the story of how we began turning battlegrounds into playgrounds.

PART ONE

Terror No More

*O L*ORD*, you hear the desire of the afflicted;*
you will strengthen their heart; you will incline your ear
to do justice to the fatherless and the oppressed,
so that man who is of the earth
may strike terror no more.

PSALM 10:17-18 ESV

1

The Girl with Pink Ribbons

*Greater love has no one than this, than to
lay down one's life for his friends.*

JOHN 15:13

There were at least 70 dead bodies strewn among the rubble on one of the avenues where Iraqis had tried to leave the war-torn city of Mosul, and in June 2017, it was a city still controlled by ISIS. In order to escape starvation, leave the city, and cross over the front line of battle, fleeing Iraqis had to navigate one final wide space. But ISIS snipers sat on top of the surrounding buildings and shot innocent people as they moved out into the open road. This is a hallmark of ISIS fighters: Even in defeat, they kill the innocent and leave landmines behind in kitchen cabinets or attached to children's toys.

Dave Eubank, an American aid worker and leader of the Free Burma Rangers, looked through binoculars once again, his eyes scanning over the rubble and the area carpeted with dead bodies. Dave is someone who refuses to avert his gaze. He is always looking, and he is always asking, "How can I help?" He has become my friend—I'll tell you more about how that happened later—but this moment is important. This is a moment I need you to see.

As he stood there, refusing to look away, he saw something in the midst of all the dead bodies: movement. He saw someone moving.

"Wait! Stop!" Dave said. "What was that?"

He and his group looked closer. I imagine them passing the binoculars back and forth. There was movement again, and this time Dave got a better look. A child was hiding there, among the dead, too afraid to move because of all the gunfire. The child was safe for the moment, still unseen by ISIS, but Dave couldn't imagine that would last much longer.

"She's been hiding there for days," Dave said quietly, watching her through the binoculars. How scared she must have been! How hungry and thirsty and terrified. He could clearly see her for a moment. She wore a pink dress and had pink ribbons holding back two ponytails. She was hiding under a woman's black hijab, the long, flowing garments Muslim women wear when out in public.

What astounds me most about this scene is that these bodies, and the living little girl, had been in this position for days! People had driven by—ambulances, armed forces, soldiers, ISIS—yet no one stopped to truly see. Everyone else saw only a huge group of dead bodies, and because they looked away, they failed to see the person who needed them the most.

The story of the good Samaritan immediately comes to mind.

> A certain man went down from Jerusalem to Jericho, and fell among thieves, who stripped him of his clothing, wounded him, and departed, leaving him half dead. Now by chance a certain priest came down that road. And when he saw him, he passed by on the other side. Likewise, a Levite, when he arrived at the place, came and looked, and passed by on the other side (Luke 10:30-32).

Religious men looked but turned away. Maybe they didn't have time. Maybe they didn't want to defile themselves. Maybe they were horrified by the violence in the world. But when confronted with death and horror, they looked away.

> But a certain Samaritan, as he journeyed, came where he was. And when he saw him, he had compassion (verse 33).

When he saw him, he had compassion.

Dave saw this little girl, and compassion overwhelmed him. There was no way he could go on after that, pretending he hadn't seen her. He had to do something.

What will we do when we finally see? Will we walk by, or will we have compassion?

What happened next was caught on tape and played back by news stations all around the world, including Fox, CNN, and CNBC. And when I watch the video of Dave rescuing that child, his mission to snatch a little girl out from under the guns of ISIS, I can't help but feel like I was there with him because over the last few years I have gotten to know Dave. I know how he ticks. I can even imagine what he was thinking.

Dave Eubank is the head of a group called the Free Burma Rangers. The Free Burma Rangers (FBR) was formed in 1997 and is a multiethnic humanitarian service movement. They bring help, hope, and love to people in the war zones of Burma and now Iraq.

In a "Letter from the Director" on their website, Dave writes, "The name of the foundation is inspired by the words of Jesus in Luke 4:18-19 (NIV): 'The Spirit of the Lord is on me, because he has anointed me to preach good news to the poor. He has sent me to proclaim freedom for the prisoners and recovery of sight to the blind, to set the oppressed free, to proclaim the year of the Lord's favor.' FBR is made up of people of different faiths and all are free to believe as they choose. We of different faiths and ethnicities are joined in love as we try to serve the oppressed. For me, I want to follow Jesus in this and share His love with all in need."

For hours, Dave tried to arrange for the two things he needed in order to rescue the girl: He wanted the United States Air Force to "drop smoke," and he wanted the Iraqis to loan his group a tank to run behind. But as the hours passed, his plan didn't seem to be coming together. The US wouldn't get back to him—in a battle with ISIS, there are always more important things than the fate of one little girl. The Iraqis didn't have a tank to spare—they were already short on supplies in this fight, and they couldn't divert a precious resource like a tank for a mission such as this. Still, from morning until early afternoon, Dave petitioned on her behalf. He stood by helplessly, watching the girl, willing her to stay hidden, willing her to stay safe. He hounded any colonel or general he could find, begging them to give him the tools he needed to perform a rescue.

Dave saw the girl, and he couldn't let her go.

In the meantime, nearly everyone else around Dave was thinking, *No way! It just can't be done!* Even his closest friends were sure it was suicide to try to pull her from the group of bodies strewn through the street and the rubble. The tank could only accompany him so far—at some point he would have to run through open ground to get to her.

Why is Dave the kind of guy who couldn't let it go? Why was Dave the only one who refused to give up on that girl? It's because Dave truly believes Jesus when He says, "Greater love has no one than this, than to lay down one's life for his friends" (John 15:13). Dave believes it. He doesn't look away. And he follows through.

Dave watched as the perfect situation began taking shape. Suddenly, with very little notice, the US responded to his request, saying they were about to drop smoke on the area. At the same time, an Iraqi tank came around the corner, ready for Dave's mission. It was a miracle.

"If you're coming with me, let's go!" Dave shouted, and at the last minute, three Free Burma Rangers fell in behind him, two armed with military rifles, the third with a camera to videotape the rescue mission. The group followed the tank toward the smoke, toward the girl, toward the ISIS snipers. The tank rumbled slowly, heavily, and stopped at the location. Dave waited another moment. He peeked out to check the ground between him and the girl—it was rough terrain, a street torn up by war. His guys peeled out from behind the tank and opened up with covering fire aimed at the ISIS sniper positions. The tank fired in the same direction. And Dave made a mad dash for the little girl.

In that moment, he later said, he expected to die. He thought that was it. After all of his missions in Burma and Iraq and other war-torn countries, this dash to try to save an Iraqi girl was going to be his last.

But he didn't hesitate, because the verse kept going through his mind: "Greater love has no one than this, than to lay down one's life for his friends." What if that was his little girl? He knew he had to try.

Later, talking to news organizations, Dave said it succinctly: "I knew, if I die right now, my wife and kids will understand why. It was for the love of that little girl."

Here is a letter posted to the FBR blog, written by the Burmese cameraman who followed Dave into the fray. His nickname is Monkey.

Dear brothers and sisters,

I want to write and share what happened with God and me during our last mission in Iraq.

With every mission, after I get the call from FBR headquarters, especially for an international mission, I pray to God to make sure it is His time for me or not. It's a very simple prayer: "God, is it Your call or not? If so, I will go. If not, please give me some action to stop me." I have had confidence every time I went— except during this last time in Iraq.

This time I met very difficult situations, so that deciding to help the people in need was also difficult. I remember the time when we rescued the little girl: we saw many, many dead bodies in the main road and by the road. We also saw that some were still alive among the dead bodies. Some wounded men waved their hand for help and some children were walking, and some were playing among the dead bodies. It made me very sad, but it also made me afraid to help them. I tried to drive away the fear, thinking, What if it is my kids or family? I thought of John 15:13 from the Bible, which says, "No one has greater love than this, that someone would lay down his life for his friends." But I said in my heart, "Lord, I am not ready for this word."

I also remembered one of the mottos that all the Free Burma Rangers must follow: "Do not be led by fear or comfort." This rule also did not encourage me to do the rescue, as I am a person with fear, and lazy. When our leader, Dave, asked me, "Who will go with me?" I said, "Zau Seng" (another FBR cameraman) instead of myself. I knew many people all around the world were praying for us, but still I was weak to make the decision to go on the rescue.

When we talked about possible ways to do this rescue, we needed two things: One is the Americans to drop a smoke bomb; the other is a tank to go in front of us for our cover and to shell ISIS as well. I thought, if we got smoke and a tank, I might dare take part in the rescue. But I did not want to pray for the smoke and tank because I was not 100 percent sure I would go even then, and I had ignored answers from God many other times in my life. I could not imagine how we could get the smoke from the US Army, and the local authorities had already refused our request for a tank. But Dave did not give up. He prayed and talked to friends, and our team talked and prayed together.

Then, while we were talking about how we could do the rescue, standing in a building by the main road, a smoke bomb from the air was dropped. We stopped talking and ran down to the corner of the road. A big tank came and turned toward the main road. Dave started running and shouting, "Whoever wants to go, let's go!" and led in front.

I did not have time to think and make a decision. Only one thing I shouted in my heart, was, "This is God! He is in it."

I ran and followed the group. I could not believe that we got the smoke and a tank. The tank was even bigger than I thought. After the rescue, Toh, our medic, and Zau Seng, our other cameraman, and I stood among the Iraqi soldiers. One of them looked into my eye for a while, saying nothing, but his eyes were kind. Then he turned into the building and came back with a hat: it had S.W.A.T. on it, and he placed it on my head. "Wow, that is an honor," said Toh and Zau. I could not think too much. I was re-concentrating my mind.

That night, I reviewed what had happened and what I had done:

1. We did the rescue.

2. I refused God's Word: John 15:13.

3. I refused the Ranger motto.

4. I refused my leader's call.

5. We got what we wanted and needed, even though I personally did not even want to pray for it.

Just think. I was a part of it because of God's mercy and faithfulness. I realized the honor is His, not mine. I do not deserve it because I refused everything to do the rescue. Only because of His mercy and faithfulness to all His creation did I dare go. This is why I want to write and share with you, and give all the glory to Him.

He is very merciful and faithful to you, me, and all.

I want to thank God for His mercy and faithfulness to all of us. I want to thank people all around the world for being in prayer for us. I want to thank our team for working together as a family. I want to thank our leader for leading us boldly and in love.

God bless you,
Monkey

If you watch the video, when you see Dave Eubank run out from behind that tank, you will hold your breath. He pulls the girl out from a sea of dead bodies, out from under the black hijab of her dead mother. That was where she had been hiding for days—under the protective shadow of her mother, already gone. Did her mom, days earlier, act with the same heroics as Dave? I believe she did. I believe she died shielding her little girl.

When Dave returned to the tank, he was panting, groaning. But he had done it. He carried her under his right arm like a football, his left hand holding his helmet on his head. She was quite a bundle, and he placed her on the ground behind the tank. She had dark, curly hair. Her face was blank. She leaned over. Later there was a photo that circulated of Dave carrying her to safety behind the tank—he had picked her up again, and her arms were wrapped around him, her head tucked into his shoulder. He was cradling her the way I wanted so badly to cradle the boy in the back of the ambulance or the boy on the beach.

Dave saw, he didn't look away, and he acted.

In the scheme of life, what makes that little girl so important that her mother would die protecting her, that Dave would risk death to retrieve her? I do not know the answer to that, except that there is a Jewish saying, "If you lose a life, you lose a world." And Dave knew the answer too, because "greater love has no one than this, than to lay down one's life for his friends."

It is easy to see the atrocities in the world and be overwhelmed. I often feel it too—how can we, normal folks living normal lives in the United States, make a real difference? The world is such a big place— what can someone like me do?

What can someone like you do?

But there are "normal" people like us making a huge difference in the world. People like my friend Dave Eubank and his family. People willing to lay down their lives. Even people like Monkey who resist being involved right up until the moment something happens and then they act.

People willing not to avert their gaze but to see, and then to do.

The fact that Dave and I even crossed paths is amazing and providential. I was a pastor's wife in Albuquerque, New Mexico, and he was an aid worker leading the Free Burma Rangers from Thailand. We were thousands of miles apart, and he was working diligently, quietly, in the jungle.

When I prayed and God told me to fight for children impacted by terror, kids caught in the crossfire, I started looking at the entire world. I could have connected with any one of a thousand organizations. I could have ended up in any of the world's 194 countries. Yet God pointed me to Dave Eubank.

I feel like I won the lottery.

I was led to Dave Eubank pretty early in the life of Reload Love, around the time we chose the name for our organization. The connection happened when I got to share my idea about helping children impacted by terror with someone I respect a great deal: Franklin Graham. Skip was on the board of Franklin's organization, Samaritan's Purse, and we had done a lot of events with him. He was there in the early days of some of my various schemes and ideas—I had floated one to him right after 9/11, an idea that had also involved jewelry and my desire to help other people. So one afternoon when I was talking with Franklin, I started telling him about Reload Love, this new initiative we were starting.

I went through the whole thing with him, from reusing bullet casings to how we were making the jewelry, to my vision of using the proceeds to help children in terror (you'll find out more about all of this shortly). When I told him about the bullets, he sounded skeptical. I think at first he wondered what I was up to. He is a sportsman when it comes to guns, and I think a lot about the concept was counterintuitive to him.

"I have the bullets," I said. "And we're making the bracelets. But now I have to find babies to help. Where should I go?"

Once I started talking about helping babies, he didn't hesitate. He made a suggestion, and it would become one that shaped Reload Love. It would also prove to be a suggestion that would shape me.

"You should go to Burma," he said, belting out the name of the country in his deep, southern drawl.

"Burma?" I asked.

I wanted to ask him if he was sure we couldn't help children on the Champs-Élysées in Paris? Maybe somewhere a little more refined? But all kidding aside—can I be honest? I had no clue where Burma even was!

"Yeah," he continued. "You should go to Burma. There's this organization there called the Free Burma Rangers run by a man named Dave Eubank. He and his wife put on backpacks and run through the jungle rescuing kids and preaching the gospel. They live there with their three children. That's where you should go. Burma."

God led me to Dave Eubank through Franklin.

Franklin went on and on. I knew nothing about Burma or the Burmese conflict or the Free Burma Rangers. I knew nothing about the Karen tribe, Christians who are hidden away in the deepest recesses of the world, trying to survive.

I went home that night and started researching Burma, its history, and the people associated with it. I looked up the Free Burma Rangers. I studied the neighboring countries and the geopolitical situation. I was intrigued by the Karen tribe and the fact that they were hiding in the middle of an animist, Buddhist culture. I discovered that Laura Bush had run an initiative to help the Karen people back when George Bush was president. I thought it was interesting that we wanted to help children in terror and the war being fought in Burma was the longest ongoing conflict in the world, more than 65 years old.

Days passed and I went deeper into my studies of Burma, the Free Burma Rangers, and the Karen tribe. I had no idea there were Christians who ran toward the bullets! I had no idea people like Dave Eubank even existed.

The more I searched online, the more I kept coming across something else that caught my attention: There was a Burmese Buddhist monk who likened himself to Osama bin Laden, except he wanted to persecute the Muslim people in the country of Burma. I had never heard of that. From the perspective of a Westerner, I had always thought of Buddhists as peaceful, orange-wearing monks who chant and practice silent meditation. This particular monk's violent message struck me as strange and foreign to anything I had encountered before.

A thought slipped into my mind, the whispering of the Spirit. What if God sent me to a country where both Muslims and Christians were being persecuted? Wouldn't that be just like God? Everything about Burma intrigued me. The longer I studied this country, so new to me, the more I sensed this one word welling up in my heart: *Yes!*

That's where we ended up going on our first trip. That's where I met Dave Eubank, a man who would become like a brother to me. We would land in Dave's lap as a newborn NGO, and he would do more to shape us than anyone up to that point. That's where God began showing me exactly what He wanted me to do.

This is the story of Reload Love.

2

When I Could No Longer Look Away

Let me start at the beginning, when I could no longer look away.

This crazy journey called Reload Love began in my shower in early 2013. The shower is where most of my best ideas come to me. I think I had been watching the news the night before, and it was the first time we had seen, or at least found out about, Syria's leader Bashar al-Assad dropping sarin gas on a village. There were children living there.

I was so traumatized that someone could do that not only to people in general but specifically to children. I remember seeing the photo of a man wearing a medical mask, standing in the midst of more than 30 dead bodies wrapped in white sheets. Very small bodies. There were videos of sick children writhing in pain, weeping while groups of people tried to help them. These images from the news settled into my heart, and they churned and churned inside me, combining with a completely different experience: I had also recently been on a fashion website and noticed a cool bracelet made not out of sterling silver but out of brass. All these thoughts and images and dreams spun around in my mind right there in the shower while the warm water washed over me. I could feel my mind latching onto new ideas, poking at them, turning them over and over.

Huh, I thought. *Brass. That would probably be cheaper than sterling silver.*

Another moment passed.

Aren't bullets made out of brass? I wonder if you could make bracelets from spent bullet casings.

I wasn't concerned with my shower anymore. I had found a trail, and I was following it to the end. I thought I might be on to something.

Brass would definitely be cheaper, and using bullet cases would be upcycling. Everyone's into that right now.

I jumped out of the shower, wrapped a towel around myself, and went straight to my computer. I typed "spent bullet casings" into the search engine and scanned the results. What I found stopped me in my tracks: Spent bullet casings are available by the bucket load. Most people don't reuse them, and if you could prove you were going to manipulate them or mutilate the case so they could no longer be used as bullets, even the military would give them to you.

I called my friend Jen Santiago.

This is the heart of the matter: God can do anything. He is the God of providence. If you want to have an encounter with Him, you have to be willing to bump up against Him, keep searching for direction, keep looking. If you want to encounter God and the deep meaning He has for your life, you have to seek Him.

Even in the shower.

Then, as you seek God, instead of thinking of all the reasons something might not work, start asking different questions.

Why not me?

Why not my dream?

Why can't this thing I've been burdened with, why can't these desires that fill me, come to fruition?

> Delight yourself in the LORD, and he will give you the desires of your heart. Commit your way to the LORD; trust in him, and he will act. He will bring forth your righteousness as

the light, and your justice as the noonday. Be still before the
LORD and wait patiently for him (Psalm 37:4-7 ESV).

If we delight in God, He will put desires into our heart. He'll trans-
form our desires so that they match up with His desires. Maybe God is
calling you to feed the homeless or start a business or volunteer somewhere. Trust Him. Don't think the idea is crazy or way more than you
could possibly do.

When I have a thought like the one I had in the shower about turning bullet casings into bracelets, I stop. I commit that thought to Him.
I make a plan and start taking steps forward, and I trust that God will
open and close doors, that He will guide me along the path. There is
no pressure on me at that point, as long as I keep taking steps forward!
The onus to bring it to pass is on God. The success or failure of the venture is God's to determine! My responsibility is to keep moving.

What I've experienced in my life has led me to take the thoughts in
my mind seriously, as if they are God's thoughts, and then ask Him if
they are from Him. Have you ever had the experience that sometimes
the ideas you have in your mind didn't originate with you, that they
arrived there supernaturally? Sometimes those ideas that "just pop into
your head" are from God. When an idea drops into your brain, as if
from nowhere, realize it might not be your idea—it might be God's
idea, given to you, the person He most wants to run with it.

Ask Him.

God, is that You?

God, do You really want me to do this?

God's voice is always easily discernible because it's full of grace. The
enemy's voice, on the other hand, is also easily discernible, because all
he wants to do is to kill and destroy. He comes to us in the guise of envi-
ous thoughts, hateful thoughts, destructive thoughts. Jesus said, "My
sheep hear my voice, and I know them, and they follow me" (John
10:27 ESV).

When you hear the voice of the Shepherd, you will know it.

When you hear the voice of the Shepherd, follow it.

My friend Jen and I had started getting really close in 2008 or so.

She came to my office to work on special events and contribute toward overseas ministry efforts. She was my mission outreach director, which at the time meant raising money for the Ronald McDonald House in Albuquerque. It was important work, but that was about the extent of what we were doing, and there wasn't much life in our effort. We wanted to do more. A lot more.

As I got to know Jen better, I became amazed at how similar our hearts were for overseas missions. For years we had this desire to take teams somewhere far away, somewhere untamed, in order to see God do something bigger, something inexplicable. Something we couldn't control or take credit for. We would actually pray for this, that God would take us to the farthest reaches of the planet, blessing people and sharing the Good News with them. But as time passed, I have to admit—sometimes it was hard to imagine it ever happening.

It can be that way, can't it? If we're not careful, time will introduce doubt into our minds, doubt that we will ever do anything meaningful for the kingdom, doubt that God remembers us in our little corner of the world. But we have to be patient. Sometimes the waiting will take years. But God is always faithful.

When I called Jen that day, fresh out of the shower with this bullets-to-bracelets idea, she said one thing.

"Okay."

She has always been willing and eager to try anything, and when you hang out with me, your limits of "anything" can be tested! I hung up after spilling my idea over the phone to Jen and started combing the Yellow Pages for a jeweler we could go and talk to. I found a place down in Lomas that made silver charms, so I called Jen back to see if she'd go with me to talk to them. Yes, it was the very same day. When I hear the voice, I don't sit around and wait.

We pulled into that jeweler with literally nothing but an idea. If I tried to list for you all the things I didn't know at that point, it would fill up the rest of the book. I had so many questions, but I knew I had to keep moving forward. Just keep moving. If you wait until you know everything in order to move forward, you'll never move. Take the next step as it comes.

A woman named Molly worked at the first jeweler we visited, and she was a very nice, serious woman. I was feeling excited, the way I usually feel when a new idea is taking root and the first few steps go by without a major obstacle appearing. We told her what we were thinking, and she started explaining the process of making bracelets out of sterling silver. I let her talk for a little bit before jumping in.

"But we don't want to make them out of sterling," I said. "We'd like to do brass. Would that work?"

"Sure," she said after thinking for a moment. "That would work. We can do brass."

I could tell that the mention of brass had gotten her attention—I guess because it was kind of a different idea—so I kept going. Jen almost always encourages me to move forward, but Molly seemed like the kind of person who would shoot straight with me, someone who would say no if my idea wasn't any good. So I told her what I was thinking.

"Actually," I said, "we were thinking of collecting spent bullet casings and turning them into bracelets."

She got this look on her face, a curious kind of look, and sort of stepped back from the counter. She even teared up a little bit—there was definitely an emotional response to the idea of turning bullets into something beautiful. It was a bigger response than I'd expected, and something about her reaction nestled into my heart, made me think we might be on to something big. It's a good feeling when you share a new idea and you can tell it makes an impact.

This was still day number one.

That night Skip and I were in bed reading. He's such an encouraging husband—he really gives me a ton of bandwidth with my crazy schemes. He's willing to let it happen, to sit back and let me run ahead with my own stuff, even though we're wired very differently.

Not only does he encourage me, he's my inspiration when it comes to making courageous moves for Christ. He flew into Mogadishu with Franklin Graham and a team from Samaritan's Purse just before the Black Hawk Down incident. When they landed in the military airport and walked across the tarmac, they saw caskets draped with flags being loaded into airplanes.

Franklin turned to him. "Are you ready to die?" Franklin asked my husband. In those days and in that part of the world, death was a very real possibility.

Skip also traveled from Jordan to Baghdad shortly after the United States' "shock and awe" invasion of Iraq, accompanying trucks full of Operation Christmas Child boxes deep into territory where other NGOs had yet to arrive. Skip's always been willing to follow God wherever He is leading, and to do it with courage and faith.

I learned that from him. I learned to be obedient. I learned not to be afraid.

After I explained everything that night to Skip, from how to melt down the bullet casings to how to make the jewelry molds, he just nodded his head, following along. He wasn't going to do anything to stop me, but he also wasn't going to take the ball and run with it. He had enough going on as it was.

"Sounds good, Lenya," he said with his trademark smile. I gave him a good-night kiss, and we turned out the light. But it took me a little while to fall asleep that night. Flashing through my mind were images of brass being melted down, beautiful jewelry being made. Images of children who had been defiled by sarin gas, their bodies quivering.

Where are You leading me, God? What are You trying to tell me?

The word started to spread among our friends that Lenya had come up with another idea. One of our security guys at church heard about our project, and he just so happened to work for the city. He came up to me one day after the church service.

"Is it true you need bullet casings?" he asked. "You can come on down to the police firing range and take as many as you want. No one picks those things up."

"Are you serious?" I asked him.

"Go ahead. Knock yourself out."

That was how I found myself at the Albuquerque police firing range on a regular old Saturday morning with Jen and her kids and another family with their kids filling buckets with bullet casings. It was like an Easter egg hunt!

"Look, I found one!" the kids called out all morning.

"There are a bunch over here!" another child shouted.

We wandered from here to there, sometimes picking them up one at a time, sometimes grasping entire fistfuls, dropping them into our buckets where they made a tinkling sound, like wind chimes. At one point I reached into the bucket and lifted up as many as I could hold, then let them fall through my fingers like sand.

Could this be it? Could this be a way to help kids caught in the crossfire of terrorism? Little did I know, a few years later I'd be picking up spent bullet casings on the streets of Iraqi cities, bullets that had been fired by ISIS, bullets on streets that wrapped around new playgrounds we had built for children impacted by terror.

I had no idea where this journey was about to lead me.

More people started hearing about what we were up to. State troopers started bringing in their bullets, and sheriffs started bringing in their bullets, and sportsmen used it as an excuse to go out shooting and then brought in their bullets. The word started to spread, and soon people I didn't even know were bringing bags of spent bullet casings into our office and dropping them off.

"I heard you're collecting spent bullet casings to help kids," they'd say, shrugging their shoulders. "Here you go."

Delight yourself in the LORD, and he will give you the desires of your heart...

We had the bullets. We had the jeweler. We had a CAD designer and a manufacturer. Molly, the jeweler, helped us get the prototype made and then passed us off to a different manufacturer called Hutches. They were willing to spend a little more time playing with the casings in order to get everything just right. They tried different temperatures and other adjustments to get the brass to maximum usage.

When I saw the first prototype, I liked it. It had an organic feel, unrefined, and the brass piece was even a little dented. I thought these things would sell like wildfire once we got the word out and people heard our mission. I expected it to be like TOMS shoes, a retail success that funded our work in the field.

But I had a lot to learn.

The way I was raised, you didn't ask for money. Only people who didn't have anything, desperate people who needed something to eat for their next meal, asked for money. If God thought your life or your dream needed funds, then God provided. Our church doesn't even pass the plate to receive an offering. We simply have wooden boxes on the aisles, and if someone wants to leave money, if they want to give joyfully, they can. But we rarely ask for it.

Asking for money made me very uncomfortable, but I had a lot to learn in this regard, especially when it came to getting Reload Love off the ground. Fortunately, I had friends who would help me get over this.

A handful of us got together for lunch on a regular basis, and we just so happened to meet up for a scheduled lunch in the middle of the rise of this idea. I didn't bring them together in an organized way to solicit their help, and I didn't even plan on making the breakfast about the project I was working on, but while we sat there I started telling them about what was on my heart, how deeply I had been impacted by the children Assad had gassed, and this process I was learning about: turning brass bullet casings into jewelry.

"I just want to help kids who are being harmed by terror," I said at the end of my spiel, sighing.

I was getting excited about the whole thing when one of my friends chimed in. "Hey, I can help you with the accounting," Becky, an accountant and computer programmer, offered. I knew she was good at what she did, and I didn't have a clue when it came to accounting.

"That would be great," I said, a little shocked that she found my vision so compelling that she would donate her time.

"I love fund-raising!" another friend said. "I'll help you from that angle."

"Great," I said again. "I need help with that."

"I've put together a lot of business plans," a third friend, and Becky's daughter, Debbi, said. "I'd be happy to help you with yours."

I couldn't believe it. I was walking forward, and God continued putting people in my path to help me with each step. For a moment I sat there speechless. All their enthusiasm and offers of support felt incredible.

But as quickly as I felt myself flying away with hope when they promised to help, their next suggestion brought me back to reality.

"You're going to need some seed money," Debbi said. "You need a chunk of money to get you off the ground and pay for up-front expenses. That way you can start with a strong brand and some materials to get the word out. It's a good idea, Lenya, but you have to get it right in the beginning."

That made sense to me.

"Okay," I said. "Like, how much money are you thinking I should have?"

I really had no idea. If forced to guess, I probably would have said five or ten thousand dollars. Something along those lines.

"I would raise a minimum of $100,000," she said matter-of-factly.

That amount echoed around the room and inside my head. A hundred thousand dollars? She might as well have said $1 million! Or $10 million! I was surprised. Incredulous. Why would I need that much money? And where in the world would I get it? I certainly didn't have it.

I look at everything in life as a little bit of a challenge, and I think they could see my mind spinning. I won't say her dollar figure discouraged me, but it certainly got me thinking. They could all tell I was trying hard to figure out where I could get that kind of money.

"Don't worry, Lenya," they all said, smiling. "We'll help you raise your first $100,000."

"Really?"

Our conversation went on for a long time, and they said they would help me raise the seed money if the church contributed $10,000 toward the first trip, wherever we decided to go. I hadn't even thought of a trip yet, but it made sense—they thought I should go and visit the children, whomever it was we decided we could help. Fair enough. So I had to go into Skip's office and tell him it was getting real. This crazy idea of mine I had in the shower was going to happen. We were going to take spent bullet casings and turn them into jewelry to help children. And I was going on a missions trip—destination unknown—to help children impacted by terror.

And I had to ask him for $10,000.

At that time our church's international missions arm was in transition, and leaders were switching positions. As Skip and I discussed my idea and the need for $10,000, and as we dug around in the missions department trying to figure out how we could creatively fund this first $10,000, someone came across an old account that had been set up to receive donations earmarked specifically for, guess what?

Helping children.

The funds were in an account that had not been spent. Those funds were just sitting there, waiting for someone with an idea that was meant to benefit children. I barely even had to ask for the money. It was like God had placed it there, waiting for me to make my way through the process and find it.

I never stop being surprised at the goodness of God. I never stop being surprised at how, when He asks us to take a step of faith and when we finally take it, there He already is, waiting for us. He is both the sender and the one who welcomes us.

The summer came to a close, and what a summer it was. Before I knew it, we were almost at Thanksgiving. We had just about finalized our first piece of jewelry. We had found our first $10,000 and were busy trying to get this fledgling organization to raise $100,000. I had two main things I needed to do: name the organization and figure out where our first trip would be.

At first I leaned toward calling this new organization Bullets for Babies. I wanted something edgy, a name that would stick in people's minds and not let them forget it. I didn't care that much, or at all, about being politically correct or smooth around the edges. In fact, I kind of liked that whenever I told people my idea for the name, I got the same cringing response.

"What?" they'd ask, and they'd shake their heads in discomfort. "Lenya, that's too caustic. It's almost obscene." Really? I wanted a name that stood out, and Bullets for Babies got the kind of response I wanted. People certainly wouldn't forget it. But because people I respected had such a distaste for that name, I kept thinking up new ones, trying to come up with something perfect.

But nothing sounded right.

One night I was at the theater with my son, Nathan, the creative genius in the family, and we were chatting before the movie started. I bounced names off of him, and I was so fixated on my own names that it was hard for me to take suggestions from him. We're both the kind of people who think, *My ideas are the best ideas*, so you can imagine how that conversation was going! I would say a name and he would shake his head. Then he would say a name and I would dismiss it.

"What about Bullets for Babies?" I said, yet again, and he rolled his eyes.

"C'mon, Mom," he said. "We've been over that one a thousand times."

We sat there in silence for a minute. I began to wonder if picking a name sometimes meant choosing something you weren't crazy about. Maybe it just had to be functional. Maybe I didn't have to love it. Then my son spoke up again.

"Mom," Nathan said. "You're reusing the bullet casings, sending out love, all that kind of stuff. You should call it Reload Love."

At first I wasn't sure, but the longer I thought about it, I realized he was right.

Reload Love was the perfect name.

Perhaps the most important thing that came out of our early efforts was confirming our mission, and it became a kind of manifesto for us:

> *We are the army of love. Our mission is to convey God's love by fighting back with tenderness to children who have been impacted by terrorism. We rally as many people as possible to join our lovement to arm children with hope.*
>
> *By igniting a fervency for compassion and persuading people that one small action can make an enormous difference, we inspire others to fight beside us wielding the most powerful weapon of all: their hearts.*

But that wasn't all. We were also united behind a concrete vision. I didn't realize it at the time, but this vision would become crucial in the following years as we tried to determine our identity and whom to partner with:

> *Babies and bullets don't mix. When a crisis caused by terror arises, we send aid to in-country partners that have expertise in*

rescuing children from harm's way and provide much needed assistance, including relief supplies, children's programs, and safe spaces such as playgrounds.

Reload Love defines terrorism as unlawful acts of violence against deliberate targets with disregard for the safety of civilians or noncombatants for political or religious purposes. Whether one is for or against guns, violence, or war, we believe all can unite around the message that babies and bullets don't mix.

Reload Love raises awareness by collecting spent bullet casings. We melt them down and upcycle them into beautiful brass pieces, symbolizing God's redeeming love for oppressed and orphaned children due to the ugliness of terrorism.

We soft-launched with the women's ministry in 2013, and at first people didn't get it. They didn't understand.

"Why are you collecting bullets? How is that helping?"

In my mind I think I was so far along in the process that it was difficult for me to understand the hesitancy. But many people literally had a visceral response to the bullets part. I think the political tension in the US over guns found its way into what we were trying to do. Melting down bullets for some people hit too close to home. I guess it was too intense.

I'll tell you what I told them.

"In this country we may not all agree politically about gun control or other things like that, but can't we all agree, from any perspective, that bullets and babies don't mix? We're taking used bullets. We're making jewelry. We're helping babies. That's it. No ulterior motives."

It seemed so straightforward to me. After all, "Pure and undefiled religion before God and the Father is this: to visit orphans and widows in their trouble, and to keep oneself unspotted from the world" (James 1:27). Why wouldn't someone want to support something that is right there at the center of the gospel? Helping orphans is "pure and undefiled religion"! What could possibly be wrong with that?

We kept moving forward.

In those early days at Reload Love, we kept saying yes as long as

God was saying yes. We kept pressing forward through each obstacle. James 4:8-10 says, "Draw near to God and He will draw near to you. Cleanse your hands, you sinners; and purify your hearts, you double-minded. Lament and mourn and weep! Let your laughter be turned to mourning and your joy to gloom. Humble yourselves in the sight of the Lord, and He will lift you up."

We just kept drawing near to God. We tried to keep our hands clean and maintain humble hearts. We kept asking questions, trying the next door to see if it would open.

And they did. The doors kept opening.

We had a name, our team was growing, and that initial funding was coming in.

But we still needed to know where in the world we needed to go to help children impacted by terror. Where would be the first place God would send us?

That's when I had my conversation with Franklin.

That's when I realized God was calling us to Burma to meet Dave Eubank and the Free Burma Rangers.

PART TWO

To Every Generation

*I will sing of the mercies of the L*ORD *forever;*
With my mouth will I make known Your
faithfulness to all generations.
For I have said, "Mercy shall be built up forever;
Your faithfulness You shall establish in the very heavens."

PSALM 89:1-2

3

Through ISIS Tunnels

April 2017

Our van flies down the two-lane road, going 80 mph, 90 mph, 100 mph, and everything shoots past in a blur. I look out over miles and miles of green wheat fields, not quite ready for harvest. Isolated buildings dot the open landscape, burned out and destroyed. It's a post-apocalyptic scene, a strange and sad sight. A mountain range lies off in the distance, almost purple in the hazy, overcast afternoon.

I have to keep pinching myself.

I am in Iraq. Again.

Our van approaches another checkpoint and pulls off to the side, the gravel crunching under the tires. We are 30 minutes from Mosul, a city still occupied by ISIS. We are two kilometers from the Syrian border.

I think back to the landmine test our team had to take before we came, a test put together by the UN and required by our hosts before we were allowed to travel into the more dangerous areas of Iraq. I was at home when I read the material and took the test, and I remember thinking, *Oh, Lord.* The test opened my eyes to things I had never thought of before. In the material we learned not to pet stray dogs because they could have bombs inside of them that exploded when you touched them. We learned that if your car breaks down on the road, don't get out. We learned never to pull the vehicle onto the shoulder.

I remember thinking, *This is what Iraqi mothers and fathers and children have to think about every single day. The things I had to learn for this trip? That is what life is like for them, all the time.*

All of these thoughts go through my mind as we pull onto the shoulder of the road and our driver gets out to talk to the soldiers at the checkpoint. I wonder if it's safe to park on the shoulder. I wonder if we should be here. Our team is silent in the van, waiting for our driver to come back and tell us if the soldiers at the checkpoint said yes or no. He is talking with them, and they all laugh. He claps one of them on the back and they laugh again.

Our driver's name is pronounced "Shocker." He is tall, broad-shouldered, and his head is shaved clean. He seems to know every single soldier at every single checkpoint we come to. He was once involved with the Special Forces.

He comes back toward the van, smiling, and he opens the door.

"Let's go, everyone," he says in the voice of a drill sergeant.

"What were you all laughing about?" I ask as we climb out of the van and stretch. "What did you say to them?"

He gives a loud laugh. "I told them you're Daesh."

He pauses.

"You know, ISIS. I told them you were ISIS." He laughs again.

"What did they say?" I ask him, smiling, taken aback. I didn't think you were supposed to joke about stuff like that. To me, it felt like walking into an airport and shouting, "I have a bomb!"

"They thought it was funny," Shocker said. "And one of them said the passenger in the front seat is too pretty for ISIS. Follow me. The soldiers said it's okay. They will let us go into the ISIS tunnels."

He slams the door. He likes to joke around. This time, though, he's not kidding.

We are about to enter ISIS tunnels.

Earlier in the day, one of our hosts mentioned they had taken a friend of mine, Dick Furman, to see some ISIS tunnels. He was a vascular surgeon we had traveled with in Rwanda during the mid-'90s, immediately following the Hutus and Tutsi carnage that ended with 1,000,000 deaths. During that trip to Rwanda, he showed me where the dead bodies had been cleared from our guest house in Kigali. He warned us about where decomposing bodies were still located on the grounds. Dick was a friend, we had seen a lot together, and if he had gone into the ISIS tunnels, then I wanted to do it too.

"Are you serious?" I said, excitement in my voice. "Dick went into ISIS tunnels? If he did it, I want to do it!"

I guess they didn't really know who they had with them in the van. They looked back and forth at each other nervously. I don't think they would have brought it up if they thought I would be so interested in going.

"That decision is way above my pay grade," our host said with a straight face. "I'll have to check with my boss on that one."

For the rest of the morning I didn't let it go. I wanted to go into the ISIS tunnels.

I guess one reason I wanted to do it was simply my personality. Sometimes I have to wonder about myself! My mom had a famous saying when I was growing up. After I did something most sane people wouldn't do and she found out about it, she would ask me, "Did you not think about that?"

Sometimes when I'm at home, I jog down in the Bosque area of Albuquerque on trails that run through the shadows under the freeway, down where the homeless people live. I think it's exhilarating. My friends ask what's wrong with me.

"Don't you know women get raped there?" they ask me. "There was a knife attack there recently. Did you not think about that?"

But I don't find it threatening at all. I've hiked into the jungles of Burma. I've worked in a city on the border of Jordan and Syria. I've walked on a mountain ridge only to find out the next day that overnight the very place we had walked was targeted by a missile strike. I did all of those things for the same reasons I begged our host to take us to the ISIS tunnels. I have always wanted to look the darkest evil right in the face.

We prayed for years against the black flag of ISIS, the black banner that spread like a tumor through the Middle East. We prayed every day that a different banner would rise up, a banner of love and of the Lord Jesus Christ. So I kept asking them if we could go in the tunnels because I wanted to see a place where those black banners were no longer raised.

Our hosts kept hemming and hawing. Finally, they agreed.

"We can take you there, but we'll still have to ask at the checkpoint," our host said. "The Kurdish soldiers might not let us back there. It depends on who's there."

Now we are about to go in. We walk away from the van, and something about it feels like that scene in the movie where everything starts to go bad. The soldiers lead the way, and as is usual in Iraq, almost every soldier at the checkpoint is wearing a different uniform. There are so many groups vying for control in the vacuum ISIS leaves behind. It's hard to keep all the various forces straight: the Kurdish soldiers, the local militias, the PKK (the Kurdistan Workers' Party), the Iraqi army, and forces with ties to Iran or Turkey. This all adds to the feeling of instability. I never knew with complete certainty whom we were dealing with, what their angle was, or what their motivations might be. I trust our hosts, but all of these soldiers carry rifles. They can do whatever they want with us.

As we walk up, I see some mechanical things lying around, large pieces of equipment and tall structures that look like silos. Off to the left there is some kind of old air-conditioner or generator, rusty, and something on it flapped in the wind, making a loud, metallic banging sound.

Bang.

Bang.

Bang.

It just keeps going the entire time we're there, always off in the background. It gives me such an eerie feeling, along with the abandoned buildings, the empty fields. It feels like everyone on earth is gone except for these soldiers, the ones leading us through the wasteland.

Our hosts follow close behind the soldiers, and then there's my Reload Love team. Honestly, I can't think of them without tears of appreciation. There's Murray, our Australian shepherd-turned-guitar-playing playground builder and spiritual warrior. He told me on the plane that he had purposed in his heart to speak the name of Jesus everywhere we went. He did it the entire trip, spoke out the name of Jesus, reminding himself and us that we were there in the name of the Lord. There's Nick, always carrying his camera, always tripping over his own two feet, always willing to laugh at himself, and, most importantly, always capturing incredible images that spread the word of what God is doing in and around and through Reload Love.

And then there's Jen. Dear Jen. She is a prayer warrior, an intercessor par excellence. She is one of the godliest women I know, both in her personality and her interests. She was my husband Skip's assistant for a few years. She is a worship leader.

She is that friend the Bible speaks about, the friend who sticks closer than a brother.

All of us follow the soldiers away from the van, away from the road, and the test we took about landmines and IEDs whispers in my mind again.

Don't pet stray animals.

Don't leave the road.

Don't walk on the shoulder.

Don't pick up any debris or things lying on the ground.

Don't go inside houses that haven't been cleared.

Rocks piled on top of each other can be the locals' way of pointing out dangerous areas.

Spray-painted red Xs can identify uncleared zones.

But louder than all of those words in my mind are the famous words of C.T. Studd: "Some wish to live within the sound of a chapel bell; I wish to run a rescue mission within a yard of hell."

I've always thought that if you're going to have a mission, go right up to the gates of hell! I want the high-hanging fruit, not the low-hanging fruit. Anyone can walk up to a tree and pick the low-hanging fruit, but there are fewer people with the drive to climb the tree, to scramble up into the thick of it. I want to go where no one else wants to go, to help the people no one else has helped.

Maybe that's you. Maybe you need to stop grabbing the low-hanging fruit in your life.

We'll show them we're not afraid, I think as I follow the soldiers away from the van and into the field. *Bring it on.*

We walk back under what looks like a series of fertilizer containers—large, steel storage towers with ladders and conveyor belts and chutes. Or maybe it's used to process and move gravel. We walk farther away from the road, out into the open, and suddenly we can see forever, out into the green fields. All of these fields. All of this wheat.

There are large mounds of dirt, and at first I think they are natural hills in the field, but later I realize they are the piles of dirt made by forced laborers as they dug these ISIS tunnels and spilled the contents onto the edge of the plain. I wonder who worked for them. I wonder if they are still alive. I wonder if these ISIS soldiers were captured, what happened when this area was taken back. There is a wheelbarrow resting off to the side. There is a shovel still sticking into the rocky soil like a flag at the summit of Mount Everest.

We stumble over rocks and wade through deep grass. One moment I look up and see the soldier leading the way. The next moment I look up and he has disappeared.

Then our hosts are gone too, and I see they have vanished behind a canvas curtain that covers an entrance in the side of one of the larger mounts. It flaps in the breeze blowing around us. It's held in place by a large iron bar that lies across the top of the tunnel opening. I pull back the curtain and descend into the darkness.

I am surprised by the tunnels, surprised that I can stand up. I guess when I first heard them use the word *tunnel,* I thought we'd have to army crawl on our forearms and bellies through the dust. But inside the tunnels, even the tallest of us walk at full height. I keep ducking my head, but that's more a natural response than a requirement. I am surprised I don't feel more claustrophobic. It's all much bigger than I expect.

The tunnels feel dank, maybe because of the rainy, overcast day we left behind us at the surface. The smell inside the tunnels is like wet earth turned over. It felt like we were so hidden that someone could be walking through the field above us and never know we were there.

How often do we miss the reality of what's just below the surface?

As I continue down into the tunnel, I feel a sense of camaraderie with my team. I am right here, in this moment, nowhere else. The walls are bizarre in their perfection, covered in a series of random chisel and shovel marks. We turn on our phone flashlights, which seems weird, bringing that technology with us into a place that feels somehow ancient. Shocker wears a head lamp. We stumble farther into the darkness, talking nervously to each other, one moment laughing, the next moment silent. Here, the tunnel offers a choice—we follow our guides to the left. Then it offers another choice—we go right.

Our cameraman, Nick, is excited, and in his excitement, it feels to me like he has lost his connection with the real world. He is gone, through the lens, down the rabbit hole. I find myself wanting him to be more careful.

"Watch it, Nick! Careful! Watch your step!"

But his mind is focused on the task at hand, focused on capturing images.

Our hosts have our back. These soldiers will protect us. Part of me is nervous, yes, but I am also excited.

Let's take this territory back! I am Joan of Arc, riding into war with used armor and a spare horse! Let's do this!

We walk slowly now, trying not to trip over the person in front of us. Our lights bob along in the inky black. Shocker calls out to us, and his voice is muffled by the tons of earth around us. We catch up and see he has stepped into a side room. The walls are still dirt, but the floor has been covered in some kind of white material—cardboard? Canvas? It is hard to tell. He explains that the room is where ISIS soldiers rested while they dug the tunnels. Maybe their laborers slept here as well.

We stop and make a video for the folks back home. I am standing beside one of the soldiers. The light from the video camera is bright in that tiny room.

"Hi, this is Lenya from Reload Love, and right now we're in one of the tunnels ISIS built outside of Qaraqosh. They embanked themselves in this field, sometimes to get ahead of the battle, sometimes to sneak in and sniper the people. We have walked through an elaborate set of tunnels to get to this point. It's been an intense day. A sobering day, seeing how evil came upon this city."

The camera lights go out. We stand there for a moment, and I can almost see the men lying on the floor, exhausted from digging, some being held against their will. Again, it hits me. I am in Iraq. I am standing in an underground tunnel only miles from where a battle is raging. How did I end up in this place? How was it that God brought me, Lenya Heitzig, to the Middle East?

We go back into the tunnel, farther along, deeper in. It is easy to imagine that the tunnels go on forever, branching out like the roots of a tree, spreading through every corner of Iraq. I wonder where the branches we didn't follow would have led us. I wonder what's out there in the darkness.

Our hosts stop us.

"Has this area been cleared yet?" one of them asks Shocker. What he means is, has anyone been in this area to make sure there are no landmines or improvised explosive devices?

"Can we take them all the way to the house?" someone else whispers.

He is not sure. They have a hushed conversation between them. We are standing at a ledge—here the tunnel drops two or three feet and then continues on. Is the ledge there because they dug from opposite ends and met imprecisely in the middle? Is the ledge there for different reasons? At the bottom of the ledge is a broken fan, the kind you turn on in the summer to circulate the air, and a large, square rock. Beyond that, natural light filters into the tunnel, but I can't tell where it's coming from. The men whisper to each other. The soldiers are not with us anymore. I wonder where they have gone.

"I think it will be okay," one of our hosts says. Shocker seems uncertain, but there is something in me that wants to follow the tunnel all the way to the end. We decide to move forward. Shocker holds my hand and helps me down the ledge. I keep walking and can hear him helping each person behind me.

"Don't step on the flat rock," he says in a voice that sounds suddenly weary. I wonder if it's weighed down by all the friends and family this war has taken from him. "Don't touch the fan!" he nearly shouts at each person he helps over the ledge.

"Don't touch the fan!"

His concern is disconcerting, but we keep going. I follow them to that end of the tunnel, and I feel like we are ants on parade. Suddenly there are rays of daylight coming down from above us. There is a hole in the ceiling of the tunnel. I look up.

I see the inside of a house. The inside of a room. I can't see any details because it is dim, unlit, and the outside light is still gray, but there it is: the inside of a house. Perhaps the beginning of this set of tunnels. If you were outside looking at the house, you would have no idea the network of tunnels that stretch out in all directions. You'd never know all this is down here.

"You never know what one of their entrances will look like or where it might be," one of our hosts say. "It could be in the side of a hill, covered with trash. Or, like this, in the floor of a house."

I wonder who lived here. I wonder if they will ever come back.

We double back, changing up our order, some people passing others, some people waiting. We start to file out. I am walking with Shocker, and I point out to him a screwdriver sticking out of the wall.

"Don't touch that," I say, only half joking.

He yanks it out of the wall. I wait for the explosion that will take us all out.

"I put that there as a marker," he says, smiling. I laugh.

"Of course you did."

We head back out the way we came, but in the darkness, underground, it is easy to get confused. I have a sense that if I wasn't with our hosts and I made one wrong turn, I could get very, very lost.

"Do you want to go out the easy way or the hard way?" Shocker asks me.

"The hard way!" I say without hesitating.

And suddenly, here we are, facing the hard way out. Shocker is in front of me, and Murray is behind me. Shocker reaches up with both arms and slithers out through a hole in the ceiling of the tunnel. I am amazed at his level of fitness, that he can pull himself out like that. I didn't realize the hard way out meant pulling yourself up with no footing below.

"Uh," I say, chuckling. "I can't do this. I have no pull-up muscles!"

Shocker's arms come down through the hole and I grab on.

"Lenya," Murray says, and there is a hint of embarrassment in his voice. "I'm going to push your bum."

"Don't worry about it," I say, and between Shocker pulling and Murray pushing, I am dragged out of the tunnel like dead weight, laughing the entire way. Murray pulls himself up behind me.

Back up into the fresh air. Back up into the wide-open spaces and the fields rippling in the wind and the sound of that metallic banging.

Bang.

Bang.

Bang.

I stand up and dust myself off. We walk back toward the checkpoint, through the storage silos, and past the empty buildings. I think to myself, *This is what we prayed for, to walk on land that has been freed from the black banner, to raise a banner up in Jesus' name.*

Behind me, just a bit louder than the wind that whips the plain, I can hear Murray talking.

"Jesus, Jesus, Jesus."

4

The Ministry of Presence

Off we went to Burma.

I can't count the number of times I kept hearing Franklin Graham's voice in my mind, the proclamation he had made in his southern drawl: "You should go to Burma!"

But that's exactly how four of us from Reload Love found ourselves in a van crisscrossing the Far East on a mission to find an overseas partner who fit our criteria of helping children impacted by terror. Our trip would take us to Cambodia, Thailand, and even over the border, into Burma.

We had decided to save Dave Eubank and the Free Burma Rangers for the end of our trip, so we started in Cambodia, visiting with quite a few organizations that worked to fight child trafficking. We were impressed. They did some incredible work. Meeting some of the children impacted by human trafficking broke my heart.

We had funded a playground in Poipet, Cambodia, with a group called Mercy Ministries, long before we had examined the power of building playgrounds for children who had experienced trauma. At the time, it seemed like a random project, but one we were happy to help with. I found myself asking God, *Is this who we're supposed to help?*

As horrific as trafficking is, I knew God called Reload Love to aid child terror victims. I had researched long and hard to find a definition of terror, and we desperately wanted to keep the tip of our spear sharp and our focus clear. We felt that we had been crafted as an arrow, and our target was helping children impacted by terror. It felt to me that if we deviated from that mission even slightly, we would lose our way. We helped the organizations we visited as much as we could, but we knew that we were looking for someone different to partner up with long-term.

We swung into Thailand and walked through some schools and orphanages, but again I realized these were not victims of terror, and those were the children we were being called specifically to aid. I had to keep telling myself that over and over again, because there were good people doing good work, and the children were so precious. I learned something very quickly on that trip: In communities torn to shreds by poverty, where there is no money, children become a commodity. I would see this time and time again as our travels expanded into other parts of the world, and it would break my heart every time.

To be completely honest, by the midpoint of that trip, I was feeling slightly deflated. Before we had left, I thought we would hop in a plane, head to the Far East, and immediately find an organization we could partner with. But as the days passed, and as we visited organization after organization that didn't quite fit, I started to wonder if we actually would find someone to partner with, someone who was working with children impacted by terror.

At the very tail end of the trip, it was finally time to meet with Dave. By this point, he had taken on mythic proportions in my mind, as had the Free Burma Rangers. Their determination, their perseverance in the face of the world's longest ongoing civil war, their dedication to helping the tribes in Burma—everything about them intrigued me.

We flew into Chiang Mai, the largest city in northern Thailand, with a population of around a million people. We landed and walked through the airport. I remember that I had on a skirt and golden Espadrilles shoes, and we were about to meet the famous Dave Eubank, the head of the Free Burma Rangers. I had imagined we'd leave the airport with Dave and his crew, find a hotel, get settled, and then start talking with Dave about what he did and how we might be able to help.

The four of us from Reload Love (Jarrett—a church missions pastor—Jen, Becky, and myself) had our little suitcases on wheels, and we were waiting just inside the glass doors when Dave Eubank came striding in like a general. THE Dave Eubank. He had the swagger, composure, and confidence of a man who was comfortable in any environment. He also traveled with a posse, so he was surrounded by a group of his Free Burma Rangers. Trailing along and having a swagger all their own were his three children. They stood tall and confident.

I'm sure he sized me up, in my skirt and golden shoes, and immediately thought, *What have I gotten myself into? This is not going to happen.*

Introductions happened in a flash, and before we knew what was going on, these guys grabbed our stuff, led us outside, and tossed all of our belongings into the bed of a pickup truck already piled high with other things. There wasn't a lot of regard taken for stuff. Jen and I looked at each other, wide-eyed, laughing quietly. The whole FBR team jumped on the back of the truck and hung on, the truck sagging under their combined weight. There was a van waiting for those of us in the Reload Love team, so we piled into that. Dave slipped into a jump seat that faced backward just behind the driver, and all I could think about was the scene from *Apocalypse Now* where the sergeant walks up to the new recruits in Vietnam while a red sun rises, surrounded by smoke and the sound of helicopters, and says in a hoarse voice, "I love the smell of napalm in the morning."

If Dave would have said that, I wouldn't have been surprised. Not one little bit.

The van took off into Chiang Mai traffic, and Dave began giving us an overview, a history of his involvement in the region. He told us about the conflict in Burma, how long it had been going on, and what he did on a daily basis. At one point he told us our driver had killed people with his bare hands during their defense of Burma tribespeople. But he didn't say it in a bragging or proud manner—it was a statement of fact.

My jaw dropped open wider and wider.

Who is this guy? And what am I doing hanging out with the Free Burma Rangers?

The whole thing was this wonderful, horrific, adventurous, bouncy drive, and there Dave sat the entire time, not an ounce of fat on him, all sinews and muscle, relaxed, as if we were on a drive through rolling hills. We were the soft Americans asking if we could please pull over and get a Coke and some Pringles even though he probably hadn't eaten yet that day. That whole first leg of the journey was crazy, and soon we were driving slower but making nauseating twists and turns on roads in the back country.

I heard Dave on the phone, calling ahead, and he said something like, "We can stop there. Yeah, just order cow pie for everyone."

I was thinking, *Wait. I'm hungry, but... What?*

We stopped for a quick break, and they fed us kau pai, which turned out to be some kind of unidentified meat with rice. I was so hungry, I didn't care what it was. I inhaled it. We went back on the road, and eventually we came to a small group of huts in the middle of the jungle, little bamboo structures with thatched rooves. Our van stopped.

Was this our destination?

Jen and I got out of the van and looked around. The men jumped off the truck and threw our baggage into the dirt, just chucked it off the truck and onto the ground. I was beginning to understand that things were not going to be the way I had expected them to be. We would not be spending hours in meetings with Dave talking about the history of FBR. We would not be drinking coffee and making lists of ways Reload Love could help.

Dave was giving us the real FBR experience.

"Get back in the truck," Dave said to us while also barking orders to his men. "We're just dropping the stuff off. We've got somewhere else to go first, then we'll come back here tonight to sleep."

I looked over at Jen.

"Where is the bellman?" I whispered to her, and we both laughed and got back in the truck.

I might come across as a southern California girl, but there is a part of me that is totally up for these kinds of adventures. Besides, Jen and I had been praying for years that God would send us to the "uttermost parts of the earth," and there we were! It didn't get much farther from Albuquerque than that patch of Thai jungle!

We climbed back into the van. The road wound through the dusty jungle, and the light faded. It was dusk, and we were about to make a non-permissive crossing to an internally displaced person's camp in Burma. The sky was murky, covered in a dim film of smoke—it was the season to burn the rice paddies, and a haze hung in the air. The eerie smoke somehow magnified the sun, and it was a huge, orange orb in the sky. We could have been on another planet, Mars maybe, riding into that red sunset.

We pulled up and stopped beside more huts; everything was covered in dust and dirt. People walked up to us, people who had been waiting for hours because our flight had been late and we were running behind. It was like the scene from some surreal jungle movie. The shadows got longer and swallowed everything up. By this time I was exhausted. A woman walked past us wearing an M&M's shirt, smoking a pipe. Children were huddled in their parents' arms, and a group of men sat off in the distance, assessing us, taking us in, sizing us up with their expressionless faces.

The head of that village—I'll call him Pastor—came out from the crowd. He was short, barefoot, and wore indigenous tribal garb made up of a white handwoven tunic. He wore a blue skirt tied around his waist. Later Dave would tell us this man, Pastor, had been captured multiple times by the Burmese army for protecting his own people, but he always came back to guide them. This particular group had settled in this new spot in the jungle, but, of course, Dave Eubank knew how to find them.

I started to realize that Dave knew everything anyone could possibly know about the people and the wilderness in Thailand and Burma. The inside of his head was both map and lexicon of all the tribes and people and religions of that region. He could tell you stories that would keep you captivated for days. Weeks.

I was still walking the dusty streets in my golden Espadrilles, except at that point I began to feel like Dorothy in Oz with ruby red slippers. Who were these new people around me? And where were the wicked witches or flying monkeys hiding? Was this the yellow brick road? That's literally how foreign the entire experience felt.

Dave introduced us to everyone, and more people gathered around, people with kind eyes and a heart for hospitality. This is when I saw Dave completely in his element: He took control of the situation, speaking to them in their native language, smiling and shaking hands, greeting everyone in turn. It ended up that, unbeknownst to us, we were the honored guests.

Reload Love was the program.

"Jen, sing a song."

"Lenya, tell your testimony."

The Free Burma Rangers handed out cookies, and another one of their guys led the children in a craft where they made something out of their handprint. Dave called the shots, and the rest of us simply said, "Yes, sir. Okay, sir. Whatever you say, sir."

Before I knew it, Dave was introducing me to the small crowd as the featured speaker. I stood there in my golden shoes and shared the first thing that came into my head.

"I shouldn't be here," I told them. "And not only because of how far this is from my home or how difficult it is to get here. I shouldn't be here because I should be dead."

There was a 1950s Roy Rogers western on television that always closed with a pleasant song wishing the viewer, "Happy trails to you." It's a great sentiment. Who doesn't want happy trails? After all, when traveling a happy trail, there's no reason in the world to be anything but...well, happy. In reality, all trails don't end in happy or pleasant places. At some point along the trail, the path gets rugged, slippery, a little too narrow, washed out by rain, climbs a perilous mountainside, or dead-ends at a raging river. What began as a happy trail suddenly becomes a daunting, challenging road we must learn to navigate in a new way.

Often it's hard to deal with the difficulties we face. But, as believers, must we paste smiles on our faces and feign happiness even when we're hurting? And during times of inevitable challenge, is it remotely realistic to meet them with—of all things—joy? My dad is a cheerful riser. To this day, when he gets up in the morning, he walks outside, looks at the sky, takes a deep breath, and says, "Another day in paradise." I admire his attitude, but some days when I wake up and look out the window, I sigh and feel like saying, "Another day in the wilderness."

It's not always cut and dried—sometimes we're on the fringes of the wilderness. Maybe you've experienced a sticky misunderstanding with a friend or the inconvenience of a bounced check. Perhaps the bounced check sprang from a lost job and you're wondering how to weather this financial storm. Something as simple as answering the doorbell might bring the shock of being served divorce papers announcing the end of your marriage. The ringing phone can herald news that a child has been in a car accident, or the doctor calls with disturbing lab results. Like the title of a song by Mat Kearney, sometimes we're just "One Phone Call from Our Knees."

Life is fragile. One minute we're moving at a comfortable clip, free of obstacles, full of hope and confidence, and the next minute we're dealing with a trial. My own started in July of 2009. I went in for a routine gynecological checkup. But when the doctor told me to get dressed and come into his office, I sensed something was wrong. The conversation went something like this:

"Lenya, I want you to have an ultrasound," he said.

"Well, okay. Like, in a week or so?"

"I was thinking today. We're getting it scheduled for you now."

That felt like a strange thing to do. Schedule an ultrasound immediately?

On the way to the ultrasound, I called Skip and said, "I think something's up, and I don't think it's good."

He met me at the office. As the technician was doing the ultrasound, she asked, "So who's your doctor?"

I told her, and she said, "You know, he actually doesn't do surgeries anymore."

Surgery! Why were we talking about surgery?

Then she looked at her watch and said, "Oh, look at that. It's 4:30

and your doctor told me to call before 5:00." Technicians must submit their findings to the doctor without making a diagnosis to the patient. But I could tell by her loaded comments and concern that something was very wrong.

At that point I braced myself for heartache.

The next morning the doctor called and said, "You have a grape-fruit-size tumor in your abdomen." That was bad enough, but his next words were in that put-you-on-your-knees category. "You're standing on a train platform," he said. "You need to clear the decks. The train's going to come by, and you're going to get on it. And it's going to take you places you don't want to go."

He was right about that.

That train I needed to board took me on a journey that began with "big belly" surgery to remove the tumor. Later I would deal with chemotherapy, nausea, baldness, isolation, and unparalleled fatigue. With one phone call, my happy trail turned into a harrowing, high-speed train into the wilderness.

Trials are part of the human condition and can make or break us. The book of James regards trials as opportunities rather than obstacles.

> My brethren, count it all joy when you fall into various trials, knowing that the testing of your faith produces patience. But let patience have its perfect work, that you may be perfect and complete, lacking nothing. If any of you lacks wisdom, let him ask of God, who gives to all liberally and without reproach, and it will be given to him. But let him ask in faith, with no doubting, for he who doubts is like a wave of the sea driven and tossed by the wind. For let not that man suppose that he will receive anything from the Lord; he is a double-minded man, unstable in all his ways (1:2-8).

God's purpose is to allow challenges that bring the potential for growth and strength. We determine whether we will grow up or give up, get bitter or get better.

Can we equip ourselves with the maturity, wisdom—and even

joy—to please God during difficult times? To accomplish this, we need to understand the nature and purposes of trials.

A trial can be one of the sharpest tools in God's tool belt. He routinely uses them to hone and shape our faith. While we try to avoid them, we should expect trials. Does that sound pessimistic? It shouldn't. Jesus never said we would escape trials and troubles. On the contrary, He said, "In the world you will have tribulation; but be of good cheer, I have overcome the world" (John 16:33).

James told us to count it all joy *when* we fall into various trials—not *if* we fall into various trials. Experiencing a trial doesn't mean there's something wrong with you; it simply means you are subject to the human condition.

I didn't say all of those words in the village that night—it can take a long time to give a message when every sentence is translated—but I wanted them to know that even though they were experiencing trials worse than I'll ever experience, it didn't mean God didn't love them. I told them about my journey through that illness. I looked around as my words were being interpreted, and I could see the connections being made. Their eyes stared back at me, dark eyes, full of so much pain and determination and even hope.

"God saved me from cancer, perhaps in order to keep me alive so that I could come here and encourage you, and receive encouragement from you. Of all the surprising places in the world, He sent me here tonight to simply remind you that He loves you."

I marveled at how much God showed His love to these people, tucked away in a forgotten place in the world. He had good thoughts toward them. He had plans for them, a group of people I had never heard of, a group of people I never even knew existed. But God knew. And He didn't forget.

After I finished talking, we stayed with the villagers and ate dinner with them before making another crossing back into Thailand, driving that long, winding way to the huts where they had thrown down our luggage. Someone directed Jen and me to one hut in particular, and we pulled our dusty bags out of the dirt into our bamboo accommodations. By that point we felt like zombies.

"Throw down your sleeping bags. We'll see you in the morning," Dave said.

We were exhausted, but the ground was hard, and we didn't sleep well. Just about the time I finally fell asleep, before the sun even rose, a rooster started strutting around outside our hut, *cock-a-doodle-dooing.* Oh, and there were dozens of them in some sort of crowing contest.

Jen moaned, "Are you kidding me?" We both had to laugh.

We dragged our bleary-eyed selves from our warm sleeping bags, stretched out the kinks, got dressed, and walked around the compound of huts, finally seeing this place in the full light of day. It was really beautiful, that village, and it had a powerful history. It was in a strategic location and used as a fallback when the Burmese army had pressed into the jungle years before. It had been used as a refuge for many, and now Jen and I were taking refuge there, waiting for God to speak to us, waiting for God to show us the way forward for Reload Love. This was not lost to me, not now, and not in that moment, that God had taken us to a strategic place, a place where He would begin to reveal the next step on our journey.

As we wandered around the huts that morning and peered into the jungle, I spotted a few of the guys we were traveling with, these Free Burma Rangers, and I could tell we were moving through the jungle with highly qualified guys. They were strong and alert, calm and composed, and they moved as if they owned the entire area. I felt safe there. I realized something else as I mingled with the people and the Free Burma Rangers.

I felt strangely at home.

Later that morning my friend and president of Samaritan's Purse Canada who set up the three-country trip for Reload Love and several other NGOs, Sean Campbell, came up to me and gave me a fancy, huge, better-than-Swiss Army knife.

"What's this for?" I asked him. I was terrified of switchblades. They made me very nervous.

"You should always have a knife in the jungle," he said. "You never know when you might need to protect yourself or kill food to eat. Any true traveler in this kind of environment needs a good knife. This is your initiation."

I was definitely not comfortable with the idea of needing to kill my own food. I didn't know how to open the knife or carry it or close it, but I thanked him and hung it on my belt like an ornament. I had no plans of using it, although I appreciated the gesture. Sean walked away, and a few minutes later one of the Free Burma Rangers came over and talked to Jen and me. When he noticed the knife hanging on my belt, his eyes got large.

"Man," he said, "I don't even have a knife that nice."

I took it off my belt and handed it to him, shrugging.

"Clearly you're the guy who should have the good knife," I said, smiling.

But later Sean came back and looked at me with consternation.

"Lenya," he said in the voice a parent uses to scold a small child.

"What?" I asked.

He pulled his hand out from behind his back. In it was the knife.

"This is for you," he said seriously. "Not him."

As I continued to wander among the huts that morning, chatting with different members of the team and eating a utilitarian breakfast, I realized I had met a long-lost brother in the form of Dave Eubank. He had a true heart for people. He prayed every chance he got. He took care of his family and looked out for the tribe, always seeking the best, not for himself, but for those around him.

I also realized that I loved being in the tribe. I loved tribal life! The concerted effort to work together as a whole; the interdependence; the love and camaraderie: All of it resonated so deeply within me. I wanted a tribe to belong to!

I loved seeing how certain people in the tribe looked out for Dave's children when he and Karen weren't around. One of these people was a man named Padi, and the first time I saw him, he was doing laundry. The thing that caught my attention about him was that, even though he was caught up in the humdrum task of washing clothes, his face glowed with a calm sweetness, an unexpected joy. He moved around with a meek, quiet spirit, and I was drawn to him.

I walked up onto the porch where he was working.

"You're doing laundry?" I asked him.

"Yes," he said, nodding.

"Where do you live?" I asked him.

He picked up his backpack and smiled. "I live here."

I later found out he traveled a lot for the Free Burma Rangers. I asked him more questions about his story, and this is what I found out.

Before he met Dave, Padi was very superstitious. He believed in warnings and tokens and omens. There were days he couldn't get out of bed because of these superstitious beliefs. His life was ruled by fear.

When he came into contact with the team and with Dave, he got saved, and he called himself a one-pocket Christian because he always carried a small copy of the New Testament in his front shirt pocket. He began serving Dave's family very much like a nanny, running through the jungle with the children, watching out for them, hovering around.

During a skirmish with the Burmese army, Padi found himself in a difficult spot. He called out to God, *Lord, if You get me out of here, I'll be a two-pocket Christian!* So when he made it out, he started carrying two New Testaments, one in each of his shirt pockets. Later, during a battle when he was injured, he cried out again to God, *But, God! I'm a two-pocket Christian!*

He was delivered from fear and now clings to Christ, this two-pocket Christian. Whenever I think of the verses in Ephesians that talk about putting on the full armor of God, the helmet and the breastplate and the sword, I think of Padi and how he's a two-pocket Christian, wearing the Word of God.

After breakfast we loaded up the vehicles. It was time for a trek deep into the jungle, this time to a different village, and when we arrived everyone was sitting around, once again waiting for us. It seemed that no matter where Dave Eubank went, he was at the center of the action, the person everyone relied on in order to move forward.

The first thing I noticed in the village was that there was a clearing, and in the clearing were these huge logs that had been stripped and prepared for something, massive tree trunks that now looked like Lincoln Logs. I also noticed that there were holes dug, deep holes that went straight down into the jungle soil, slightly larger than the width of a telephone pole.

That's when we learned our team was there to help this village build a new clinic, and the huge trees were the main beams of the structure.

We all came together, and Dave explained what we were going to do and how we were going to do it. There were ropes or cables tied together, and we were supposed to get four or five of those cables under one of the logs. Then someone would slip a strong piece of bamboo through the end of each of the ropes, and, with three or four people on each side of the log, holding on to the bamboo, we would carry the logs to the correct hole. Finally, they would wrap a big rope with bamboo at the top, and we'd bum rush the pole and raise it all the way up until it clunked into the hole.

That was our work for the day, putting all these beams into place, one by one.

I realized yet again how much I loved tribal life. We were sweating and laughing and straining toward a common goal that required everyone's best effort. Old men had arrived early in the day and waited patiently for our help. Young kids ran around playing until we had arrived—after that, they sat down to watch us work. They probably could have put the poles in place without us, but that's not how a tribe works—a tribe waits until everyone is there, then works together, eats together, rests together.

That's something we don't do well in the States. We're not good at waiting. We're not good at relying on each other.

It was like a barn-raising in the Amish community, and it was glorious. The day itself was hot, hotter than I can describe, and so humid I could feel the weight of the air. There was something gratifying about it, sweating and working hard. Maybe it's because as a pastor's wife I usually get treated with kid gloves, catered to, and protected. If this kind of thing was going on at our church in Albuquerque, I'd have to convince people to let me help! But there, in that clearing in the middle of the jungle, I was part of the village. I was one part of the group, no more, no less.

When we had successfully dropped each of the massive logs into its hole in the ground, Dave let us carve our names into one of them. I scratched "Reload Love" with my new knife, the blade easily peeling away the wood. It was such an honor to be there, and even though the logs would eventually be covered by other building materials, it was cool to think that the name of Reload Love would be etched into the medical facility for decades to come. It would be there to hear the cries of people in pain and bear witness to their healing.

The ministry of presence.

The work day was long, and we stayed in that village overnight. The heat refused to let up. They had a room inside a bamboo building where the women could sleep, so Jen and I tried to settle there, but the air was too still, too warm, so I asked where the men were sleeping.

"Out on the porch," someone told me.

"I'm here for the whole jungle experience," I said, laughing. "I don't want to sleep in the protection of a hut. If you want to put me out in the brush, I'll sleep in the brush."

Dave's youngest daughter, Suu, heard my audacious claims, and she piped up. She was around 11 years old at the time and could ride bareback through the jungles at breakneck speed.

"Let's do it! Let's camp in the brush! I can make you a little shelter out there in the jungle!"

I laughed, then realized she was serious, and I said, "Maybe I'll just stay here on the porch."

The night air cooled. The sky was a kind of dark I don't often see, not even in the outskirts of Albuquerque. We were getting settled there on the porch when Dave started telling us stories about Burma, stories about the great men and women who had led to us being there in the heart of the jungle, ministering to and with the Karen tribe.

Dave told us the story of Adoniram Judson, the man known as the first US missionary. In September of 1811, he was commissioned by the Congregationalist Church to be a missionary to the East (he would soon switch to the Baptist denomination). He married his wife, Ann, on February 5, 1812, and was ordained the next day. Two weeks later, the newlyweds left on a boat called *Caravan* and set sail for India, but they weren't welcome there, and by 1813, he and his wife had moved on to Burma.

After arriving in Burma, the two of them spent more than three years learning the language. Imagine the dedication, the patience required to hold off on their mission until they were 100 percent comfortable communicating. They found a tutor and dedicated themselves to the Burmese language, studying consistently for 12 hours a day. Judson built a bamboo and thatch hut in front of his home, a traditional sort of reception area that all of the homes there had, and in April of 1819, six years after arriving, he held his first public meeting, welcoming his neighbors into that reception space. It was during this time that their second oldest child died at only eight months old.

By 1817, he published 800 copies of his translation of the Gospel of Matthew—by 1823, he would finish a translation of the entire New Testament. But his work was stopped when he was violently arrested and imprisoned for 17 months. His wife, having contracted malaria, traveled from office to office trying to secure his release. She succeeded, but soon after he was finally released, in 1826, she died. Six months later, Adoniram lost their third child.

Judson had reached the end of his rope, and he hid away in sadness and depression. He had lost so much. But soon he began traveling the jungles again, trying to escape the dark cloud that had fallen over his life. In 1834, after 24 years, Judson finished a Burmese translation of the entire Bible.

This is where our story intersects with Judson's, because during his time in Burma, in the early 1800s, the Karen tribe became a Christian people. When he first arrived, Judson discovered the Karen people worshiped a god called Y'wa, believed in a creation story strangely similar to the biblical one, and had other folktales that echoed stories found in Genesis. They even had a legend that goes something like this:

> Our book of gold that Y'wa gave,
> Our book of silver that he gave,
> The elders did not obey.
> Lost, it wandered to a foreigner.
> The Karens were the elder brother;
> They obtained all the words of God.
> They did not believe all the words of God,

And became enemies to each other.
Because they disbelieved God,
Their language divided.
God gave them commands,
But they did not believe him.
And divisions ensued.

The legend goes on to say that in the beginning God had three sons: the Karen, the Burmese, and the white man. The youngest brother, the white man, read the golden book and took it away, becoming educated and prosperous. The eldest brother, the Karen, believed that one day the younger brother would return and give them back the book. They can then study it and prosper.

When Judson came into the jungle and met the Karen people, they asked him for the Golden Book, the Bible.[2] He introduced the Karen people to Christ before dying of a lung disease at the age of 61.

This was the same Karen tribe we were spending time with.

"But," Dave continued, "that wasn't the end of the story."

Fast-forward to WWII and a British soldier named Hugh Seagram. He wanted to be a chaplain, but his family couldn't afford for him to do that so he became a soldier. When the Japanese began fighting Burma, Seagram led the British forces fighting there, on the side of the Burmese. He went deep into the jungle where, surprisingly, he found the Karen tribe, a group of Christians tucked away in the midst of animist and Buddhist cultures. This was 100 years after Adoniram Judson had been there translating the Bible, yet the Karen tribe had remained faithful to their Christian heritage!

"If you are with God," the Karen leaders told Seagram when he arrived in the middle of the jungle, "then we are with you. If you are not with God, then we are not with you."

It gives me the chills just thinking about it, how this must have impacted the Christian Seagram, showing up in the farthest reaches of the earth, only to find a people who had become Christians more than a hundred years before he arrived. It was as if they had been prepared for his arrival by the work of the Judsons.

"I am with God," Seagram told them. Seagram taught the tribal people how to survive, how to fight in their war against Japan—and he worked with not only the Karen people but any who welcomed him. He transformed them into a military unit, able to defend themselves against any persecutors. But when the Japanese began a methodical manhunt and came through on their promise to kill any and all tribes people until they found Seagram, he and a few others handed themselves in.

They were executed.

"Jump forward to the '60s," Dave said, "and you'll find my father riding elephants through the jungle with tribespeople, including some of the same people Seagram had trained. My father met a man named Deegay Too, a Karen warrior, a man trained by none other than Hugh Seagram, or Grandfather Longlegs, as they called him.

"It used to take my dad six weeks to get to this village on the back of an elephant. This is where he first met a man named Pad Da Du, and because it took so much longer to get here, once my dad got here, he'd stay for a little while. The two men started up an ongoing conversation about God and the Golden Book and spirituality.

"He turned to my dad one day and said there wasn't much hope or opportunity for his people. 'See,' he said to my dad, 'we are like tadpoles in the water that gathers in the footprints the elephants leave behind. Then a palm leaf falls over the water, and the tadpole is invisible, forgotten. We are so miniscule. Unnoticed by God. How will we ever get out?'

"My dad thought about what he was saying and replied, 'But tadpoles don't remain tadpoles. They eventually become frogs. God makes all things new again! He can redeem anything, anyone, from the mire.'"

Dave paused.

"This was my father's first convert to Christianity. As the years passed, my father made further inroads with the Karen people, all because of those who came before him. It is generation after generation of God reaching out to the Karen people, providing allies who help defend them and the rest of the Burmese tribal people against persecution."

Finally, jump forward to the '90s, when Dave entered the Burmese jungle with his family and met Molah, the son of Deegay. Dave continues the tradition of protecting and upholding the native people in the Burmese jungle, including the Karen people, this Christian tribe.

I lay there on the porch in the dark, listening to Dave tell this winding, enchanted history about men and women who had come to Burma during the last 200 years. What a legacy God had created, right there in that jungle! Generation after generation of people most of us have never heard of, liberated and supported and cared for by men and women of God, sent from the comfort of their own land and homes.

And I believe this isn't just happening in Burma. In every place in the world, there is this compunction in the heart of God that we join Him, pick up the torch, carry our cross, and move forward, carrying His faithfulness to every generation, in every land.

I felt so small, standing in the shadows of Judson and Seagram and the Eubank family. What was I doing in the jungle, following along behind such giants of the faith? But I realized I was doing something, something important: I was practicing the ministry of presence. I was sitting with this passage of history and witnessing the faithfulness of God. It made me love God even more.

I realized He can do anything for anyone in any generation.

> I will sing of the mercies of the LORD forever;
> With my mouth will I make known your faithfulness
>   to all generations.
> For I have said, "Mercy shall be built up forever;
> Your faithfulness You shall establish in the very heavens"
>   (Psalm 89:1-2).

We all slept outside that night on the porch. I figured that at least there, in the fresh air, it wouldn't be so stifling. Jen and I got settled in our sleeping bags and drifted off. Well, wouldn't you know it— at night it was freezing cold! I'm not sure I slept for more than a few minutes at a time. Jen and I ended up hugging each other, trying to stay warm.

They were long, cold nights and hot days. It was the incubation period for Reload Love, and in many ways the incubation period for me and the rest of the team in this new mission. I felt an underlying sense of excitement for what we were doing and for what was to come. I felt that God had led us to Burma, and I was so eager to see what would happen next.

5

Run into the Roar

We returned to our home village with Dave and his crew the next day, and I was in dire need of a shower. We had been on our Far East trip for a week, and this was our second full day with Dave. Our time with him had been spent hiking and working nonstop. I'm sure you can imagine the state we were all in. I asked Dave about the possibility of getting a shower, and he nodded.

"Peter!" he shouted, and his eight-year-old son came running through the huts. If you want to know who Peter is and what he's like, I have one word for you: Mowgli. You know, the character from *The Jungle Book*, the boy who scampers among the trees and talks to the animals and isn't afraid of anything? That's Peter.

"These ladies would like to bathe. Can you take them down to the waterfall?"

My eyes stopped blinking. *The waterfall?*

"Sure!" Peter shouted.

"You might want to wear your bathing suits," Dave suggested. So Jen and I gathered our small bags of toiletries, and we followed Peter out of the village, down a long hill. We walked on a narrow path through the jungle, climbing over logs and ducking under branches, and by the time we got toward the bottom, our legs were covered in mud.

"Well," I told Jen, "now we definitely need to clean up."

Peter disappeared during the last stretch.

"Peter!" I shouted. "Wait up!" We went around a corner trying to catch up to him, carrying our things and stumbling along, and then we saw it. A waterfall crashed down into deep pools scattered among boulders and rocks. We walked up to the edge of the pool they used for bathing, and it was a decent jump down into the water, maybe five or six feet. I looked over at Jen.

"Are you kidding me?"

I am not that kind of person. I am not a camper. I can't tell you the last time I jumped into a pool of water like that. I looked over at Jen and laughed a nervous laugh. She looked back at me, probably a little uncertain as to what I would do. She probably thought she was going to have to push me in.

"Okay, here goes," I said, and we counted to three and jumped, plunging into the cold water. It absolutely took my breath away.

We cleaned ourselves off in the pool of water, and then we helped each other climb out, scraping knees and elbows, and finally hiked back up the mile-long muddy trail, sweating the entire way. It turned out to be a complete waste of time, taking that "shower," because we arrived back at camp at least as dirty and sweaty as we had been before—maybe even worse. But it was new dirt.

This was life with Dave. This was tribal life in the jungle. I have to admit: I loved it.

In the midst of the hikes and the work, the new people and jumping into deep pools, I found myself asking God the same question over and over.

God, why am I here?

This work in Burma had been going on long before me, but it also seemed like a lot of what Dave was doing was coming to an end or being handed over to the local people. I could envision calm finally coming to that part of Burma, with some of the tribes even able to return to their homelands peacefully.

God, why am I here? Why did You bring Reload Love to this place?

I walked around the camp that morning and chatted with quite a few of Dave's chaplains—every team he sends out has a chaplain on it, someone whose primary role is spiritual. Someone who is seeking God no matter what they encounter. I met some of these men, and I listened to their stories, and the question always hovered in the back of my mind.

God, why am I here? Why did You bring Reload Love to this place?

And because I'm a pastor's wife, and because I'm a Calvary Church pastor's wife, and because I'm Skip Heitzig's wife, I believe the Word of God does the work of God. When you empower people with God's Word, you empower the sheep to accomplish missions for the kingdom of God.

Many of Dave's chaplains had fled to that very wilderness from other areas of Burma for their lives, some bringing their families and some coming alone. Dave found them there in the jungle and trained them and gave them purpose. They weren't all Christians, but they taught the same messages as they went from place to place as part of his teams, messages of forgiveness and love and hope. And they all knew, they all hoped, there would be a day when they could return home.

One of the ways Dave trained the men was by holding a boot camp once a year, and around 300 indigenous people flooded into his camp from all over the country, from every tribe and religion. He trained medics, and while he didn't require they become Christians, he did require they know enough about the Christian programs they ran to enable them to act as chaplains and teach gospel skits like the good Samaritan and David and Goliath.

During one of Dave's boot camps, a Burmese army member came out of the brush. Everyone was suspicious of him, but he wanted to be there and join the cause. He observed them, and they observed him. After a period of time, he said he wanted to repent and be baptized, but he didn't think God could forgive him. He had killed a pregnant woman during a village raid.

Dave ministered to him about the forgiveness of Jesus Christ, and the man was baptized right there in camp. And after going through the boot camp, the man returned to his village to implement what he had learned, both the physical medical practices as well as the spiritual truths.

This was heavy on my mind as I walked around the village that day, this idea that all of these young men would someday return home. I felt an overwhelming sense that they needed Bible teaching. They needed to learn how to read the Bible, really read it. And they needed these tools before they left. This idea grew heavier on my heart—it felt urgent to me.

The Burma sun rose higher in the sky. The air was stifling. It was one of the first times I encountered the monotone nature of village life—once you're there long enough, you realize there is time to do…what? There's no television, none of the entertainment we use in the US to while away our time. You learn to fill your time with different things: walks, talking, thinking, and all the mundane tasks required to keep a village going.

I was doing these things and kept thinking about the chaplains. But I wasn't sure how to bring it up with Dave. He's more akin to the biblical David than Solomon. He's a man who will fight the war, not a man who will stay and build the temple. I knew this, and I wondered, *How could these chaplains receive discipleship? Who will teach them?*

I've learned that when something is heavy on my heart, I have to make time to seek God, and when I do, He will often point me to a particular scripture. When we seek Him with all of our heart, we will find Him! Well, as I sought God there in the jungles of Burma, just me and the heat and the rice paddies and the huts, God spoke. "For I know the thoughts that I think toward you, says the LORD, thoughts of peace and not of evil, to give you a future and a hope" (Jeremiah 29:11).

In my mind I applied that to all the ethnic groups in Burma, all the people who had been forced to flee their homes, all the people who had hidden themselves away in the wilderness. I realized that all along there had been a plan for them. Even though they were refugees, even though they were IDPs (internally displaced persons), even though they were on the run from those who would harm them, God knew the plans and thoughts He had for them. Thoughts for good and not for evil.

I realized they were the generation to come, the people of the future for Burma. These people who had fled persecution and been trained by Dave and the Free Burma Rangers would someday return to their homes and teach their own people. I kept ruminating over Jeremiah 29:11, but Skip is always encouraging me to look at verses in their context so, for the first time in a long time, I went beyond Jeremiah 29:11 and read the entire chapter.

> Now these are the words of the letter that Jeremiah the prophet sent from Jerusalem to the remainder of the elders who were carried away captive—to the priests, the prophets, and all the people whom Nebuchadnezzar had carried away captive from Jerusalem to Babylon (Jeremiah 29:1).

The entire chapter is a letter to those who are held captive. And I was right there, with the captives! I was walking and talking with the Burmese people in Thailand who had fled their homeland.

Jeremiah went on to describe the Jewish captives' predicament, and he proclaimed a new word to them from the Lord of heaven's armies:

> Build houses and dwell in them; plant gardens and eat their fruit. Take wives and beget sons and daughters; and take wives for your sons and give your daughters to husbands, so that they may bear sons and daughters—that you may be increased there, and not diminished. And seek the peace of the city where I have caused you to be carried away captive, and pray to the LORD for it; for in its peace you will have peace (Jeremiah 29:5-7).

In other words, he was encouraging them not to waste their lives pining away for their homeland. "Build homes," he said. "Plan on staying. Put down roots. Grow a new crop. Find spouses. Have children. Multiply. Work for peace and prosperity in the city where you have been sent. Pray to the Lord for this new city, for its welfare determines your welfare."

Simply put, "Live your lives."

I looked around me, at the huts built and the rice planted and the clearings made. This is what these IDPs were doing: settling and building and living. I felt God saying, *See, Lenya? I took them out of their homeland and planted them here and now they are prospering, but someday I'll send them back. I know the plans I have for them. I know the plans I have for you. You will find me when you seek for me with your whole heart. I will end your captivity and bring you home again to your land.*

I sat there on the porch of a hut on the border between Thailand and Burma reading this passage, and God whispered to me, *This is what I am doing. You are seeing it firsthand. This is how the ministry of presence will turn itself around and minister to you.*

Emotion rose up inside of me. *My God, Your ways are not my ways. I would never ask people to do this—I would never put them through this, leading them out of their homeland and into a foreign place. But You, in Your wisdom, brought them here to hear the gospel, and to be encouraged, and to meet amazing people like Dave Eubank, and then someday to be sent back to tell their friends and family about You. In Your timing.*

Always in His timing.

I had to tell Dave about this word. I had to explain to him my vision. That night I had my chance.

At night Dave sat on his porch in the village with a light on, and people came to talk to him. There was a steady stream of visitors, sometimes in groups of two or three or four, and sometimes just individuals. He was like the village elder—they went to him to talk about their needs or to see what they could do to help. This is tribal life.

Have I mentioned yet that I loved tribal life?

I waited for a gap in the stream of people, and when Dave was on the porch without anyone else, I walked over and approached him. I was nervous; this was Dave Eubank! The legendary leader of the Free Burma Rangers. This was General MacArthur! And not more than two days ago I had come out of the airport wearing gold slippers. Why would he listen to me?

So I sat with him and told him my vision, my concern for the chaplains, my ideas about the importance of teaching the Word of God to the people. I told him the word I had received from Jeremiah 29 and the beautiful timing of God. And he listened to me, listened politely, even though he could have waved me away and said he had more important things to do. Because he did. But instead, he listened.

Eventually my words stopped coming. He looked at me there in the darkness. All around us jungle insects were chirping and clicking their strange rhythm. I could sense that other villagers were waiting for us to finish so that they could have their turn talking with Dave.

"Are you finished?" he asked, a slight smile on his face.

"Yes," I said, suddenly feeling more than a little sheepish. Who was I to tell him what to do, what to focus on? But he had listened so graciously.

"Okay," he said. He paused. Then he spoke. "I don't want to do that. I'm a soldier. The work I'm doing now, this is the work God called me to do."

"I understand that," I said. "Let's bolster the chaplains together! We can bring them CDs or mp3s. We can send them to school or bring a school here, to them. Let's do something!"

He was so patient, and he let me process out loud. We spoke for quite some time that night, and when we finished we weren't that much closer to doing what I thought needed to be done, which was creating a program to formally train the Karen tribe and the FBR chaplains in Christian theology. But I began to wonder if the vision and the word from Jeremiah had been more for me than for Dave. Maybe God was communicating a deeper truth to me, something I needed to understand and take with me in my travels to come.

Maybe God was introducing me to the concept of His timing, His faithfulness to every generation, reminding me that even in the midst of war and displaced people and terror, He is working things together for the good. After all, if He could see His own people in exile and encourage them to stay, to live, and to prepare for the day of their freedom, couldn't He do the same for all people?

The next morning Jen and I decided we would not leave the jungle until we had gone for a run with Dave Eubanks. Of course, we didn't know what we were getting ourselves into, although I should have known after what I saw during a previous late-night trek to use the restroom.

It was the second time I woke up that night and had to use the facilities, and I was stumbling through the jungle in the freezing cold, trying to find the path to the outhouse. I felt like Gilligan lost on the island. I didn't have my glasses on. I was wearing a head lamp. That's when I heard a noise under the hut where we were sleeping, and I jumped. That noise scared me to death.

But it was only Dave. Under the house. I looked closer and realized he was lifting bags of rice like dumbbells, doing curls.

"Dave, what in the world are you doing?" I asked him, my voice raspy with sleep, my eyes squinting.

"Oh," he said. "I hope I didn't startle you."

I just stared at him.

"Oh," he said again, looking down at the rice bags. "These. Well, you never know when you might have to carry someone out of here."

"Right," I said, shaking my head, the light from the head lamp swaying back and forth. "Right. Okay. Well, I'm just trying to use the facilities."

I didn't say anything else. I used the restroom and went back to bed.

The next morning Jen and I woke up for our run with Dave.

"I've got a great run mapped out for today," he said. "About four or five miles total."

It turned out that we'd be going on a path that included another crossing from where Dave lived in Thailand and into Burma.

And so it began.

The path was dry, really dry, and it was covered in a thick, red chalky powder that puffed up under every step we took. Poof! It almost felt like running on the beach. I was just a little puppy yapping at Dave's heels, and Jen was right there with me, as usual. I felt so full of energy! I was in the jungle! I was running with Dave, leader of the Free Burma Rangers! We had just crossed into Burma!

That's when I wiped out.

I tripped over something and rolled and scraped my knee, my shin, and my elbow. I went down hard. But I was not going to be defeated, especially not while running with *the* Dave Eubank. I bounced back up to my feet, trying not to pay attention to the pain. Dave and Jen were staring at me—I think they wondered if I was truly okay or if I was just playing the tough girl.

"I'm good," I said. "I'm great. Let's go. Keep going."

We continued on our run, and Dave talked the entire time, probably because he wasn't used to running at such a slow pace.

"You know," he said, "before you two arrived, God gave me a vision. In the vision God was lowering something down toward me from heaven, and I realized it was baskets. A bunch of baskets. And in these baskets were wooden two-by-fours, all jumbled up together."

We kept running, our feet clouding up red dust as we went.

"I told God, 'Hey, God, you don't carry two-by-fours in a basket. It's too unwieldy. They'll tumble out.' But the Lord continued dropping these baskets of two-by-fours at my feet. When they came all the way down, I realized they had writing on them, so I went closer and tried to read what they said. On some were written the words 'Free Burma Rangers,' and on others, 'Burma,' and on others, 'Reload Love.' All these different words."

He stopped talking. All I could hear was our heavy breathing as we ran the jungle path. It was getting warmer, but I barely noticed. All I could think about was his vision of two-by-fours with the words "Reload Love." And I wondered why so many missionaries I knew had such meaningful dreams?

"So," he said, "I know God has dropped you to me. But I don't know how He wants us to put everything together, what exactly is being made."

I don't know if I said anything in that exact moment—I was trying to keep up, trying to catch my breath—but Dave's vision fascinated me. We wanted to be in Burma. We had prayed for Sudan and the Middle East. It sounded like the words written on his boards corresponded with much of the vision we had already seen at Reload Love.

Lord, what are You doing?

Lord, what plans do You have for us?

It was an incredible week, but even after being in Cambodia and Thailand and Burma, I didn't feel that we had really connected with children impacted by terror in the strictest definition of those terms, and that was our focus. Where was God leading Reload Love? What were we supposed to do?

Before we left to go home, Dave asked us to consider another visit.

"You really should come back and let us take you into Burma, into where we train the Free Burma Rangers teams, to our main village. It's a two-and-a-half-day trek into the jungle—it's not easy to get to, not by any means. But if you want to help children impacted by terror, you should see this place. Pray about it."

"I don't know, Dave," I said. I wasn't sure. "What would we do?"

"You could help us do our big training for our Good Life Program— it's what we use in the jungle to minister to the children who've been displaced by terror and war."

That got my attention.

We became thick as thieves with Dave, his family, and FBR. It's impossible to spend time with him and not be affected by his passion, determination, and hope. He treated us as if we were a mature NGO and not the toddler organization that we actually were, and he was willing to help us achieve what we wanted to achieve. I think both of us saw there were mutual benefits to be had.

The trip home after that first Burma visit was uneventful, at least on the outside, but inside I was thinking hard and praying hard and wondering. And after we got home, Dave continued texting us, saying we needed to make the hike into his Burmese camp, the one where they did the training. He wouldn't let it go!

I wondered, *Why does Dave Eubank want us to come so badly? What is it about Reload Love that has captured his imagination and his heart? Who would want us, a fledgling NGO? What are his true motives?*

So Jen, Murray, the team, and I all prayed.

Lord, do You want us to go back to Burma?

We danced around it for a few weeks, but one night when we were all together we made the final decision: We would go back. We felt like it was the next step in front of us, the next door that we needed to push on to see if it would open. And this time we would make the daunting cross of the Thailand-Burma border and hike two days into the jungle to see how Dave trained his teams to go out and do the Good Life Program with children impacted by terror.

If you're trying to decipher God's will for your life, take a step. Jen,

Murray, and I decided we'd do it, but we didn't want to take the money from Reload Love, so we all tried to raise the money individually. And it was amazing how fast it came together. Before we knew it, I was calling Dave to arrange our next trip.

When I spoke with him, before I could even tell him we had raised the money, he jumped in. "Listen, Lenya, I think it's so important for you guys to come back and see what we're doing that I will pay for it. I will pay your way. Please just come back."

If I had any doubts about Dave or his motives, that's when I knew he could be trusted. He was willing to follow where God was leading him, even if it meant the money had to come out of his own wallet. I told him we had already raised the money. We were coming to see him again, this time in the heart of the jungles of Burma.

I knew one thing for sure: If we were going to survive that hike, I was going to have to get into better shape. Much better shape. So Jen and I joined a place called Training for Warriors. I figured if they couldn't get us ready for a trek into Burma, no one could.

The gym was located in a sketchy part of the city, under the freeway, tucked in among abandoned warehouses and crumbling streets. We pulled up to the gym, and it was not glamorous. This was not a spa. I looked at Jen, and we both smiled nervously.

"Are you ready for this?" I asked her.

"Let's do it!" she said with her trademark willingness and enthusiasm.

The place was run by a man named Vicente, and before he ran this gym he served as a Marine, a SWAT police officer, and even did some fighting in the mixed martial arts scene. We walked into the warehouse that housed the gym and looked around.

"Vicente?" I called out. There were a handful of other people working out in various corners. A guy came walking toward us: Hispanic, handsome, and in shape. Very much in shape.

We spoke with him for a few minutes and told him about our upcoming trip to Burma and the long hike we'd have to do to get to Dave Eubank's headquarters. He listened and nodded.

"Okay," he said. "Are you ready?"

If I had any notions that he would ease us into the workout, I was completely wrong. He didn't cut us any slack, not at all. In fact, the warm-up nearly killed me. We started by doing planks and burpees and jump squats. From there he led us into these things called animals—we had to get down on the floor and do a bear crawl, a lion crawl, a worm crawl. Everything was based on these funky maneuvers that used muscles I didn't even know I had. Back and forth, back and forth, Jen and I crawled on our hands and knees.

And that was just the beginning. Then came the CrossFit kinds of exercises: shaking long, heavy ropes up and down like water hoses used to fight fires. Doing exercises while carrying dumbbells and barbells. Up and down on stationary steps. Hopping back and forth for agility. Skipping through boxes drawn on the floor like hopscotch. Before long, I was sweating and, to be honest, not feeling so well.

On that very first day he lined us up in front of these heavy sleds that had weights loaded on them. Vicente called these exercises hurricanes. We had to push the sled from one end of the gym to the other. Each trip was exhausting. Each trip left me feeling like I might collapse.

Suddenly I felt like I was going to throw up.

I am not throwing up in front of Vicente, I thought, so I started scanning the gym, looking for something to throw up into or some door I could run out of. I spotted an exit. But I think he saw me and recognized the look on my face.

"By the way," he said to Jen and me, "you're training hard. Sometimes you might feel like you have to throw up. If you do, just walk off to the side. It's okay."

I didn't throw up, but I came awfully close.

Jen and I headed to this gym for one hour, three days a week, and Vicente mixed it up every time. We never knew exactly what exercises he was going to run us through. I remember one day, after an extremely intense leg workout, Jen looked over at me and whispered, "I can't feel my legs."

"It's okay," he said in the same voice he always used. He was very even-keeled, very matter-of-fact. "Take a breath. Grab a drink and get back over here."

He was nice, but he didn't tolerate any sitting out. He always expected us to hop back in and stay with it.

After spending three days with him each week, we'd take a fourth day and hike in the Sandia Mountains along the La Luz trail. Every time we went, we tried to get closer and closer to the peak. Murray joined us on those hikes, and he always made me laugh. He brought a camelback with water and a backpack full of snacks, and every little while he wanted to stop and eat!

"We're not snacking!" I told him. "We're climbing!"

On the first day, after we made it back down the mountain trail, he said, "We're going out to eat, right?"

So we went to a Flying Star, and he ordered a double cheeseburger with onion rings.

"Murray, we're supposed to be getting into shape!"

There was one thing Vicente used to always tell us that still stands out in my mind, something I thought about often during our trips to Burma and Jordan and Iraq: run into the roar.

"The world out there is a jungle," he said. "Here, with me, you're safe. But I have to train you to survive out there. Do you know how lions hunt? The female lions do the hunting, and when they find a gazelle or some kind of prey, they sneak down around the back. Meanwhile, the male lion walks to the opposite side. Once the females are in place, he makes himself known with an incredible roar, and the instinct of the prey is to take off in the opposite direction, away from the roar!"

He paused.

"But that's precisely where the female lions are waiting. Gazelles don't know that if you run into the roar, the male lion won't be able to hunt you alone, and you'll escape. Beyond him lies freedom. Beyond the roar is safety."

I think he told us this in the middle of a workout, but even though I was breathing hard and aching, I have never forgotten his words.

"You have to run into the roar."

Vicente told us stories like that every week, and it was motivating. I felt empowered, and I could feel myself getting stronger. Every single day we were there, he pushed us to our limit.

In those kinds of situations Jen gets the eye of the tiger. She becomes quiet and determined and never gives up. I am the yappy one. I either complain or fight my way through it verbally. Sometimes I get cocky. In fact, one day I started talking trash to Vicente as we trudged back and forth pushing the sleds.

"Is this the best you got?" I shouted. "Is this really all you got?"

I was kidding, of course. I thrive on keeping myself high energy. But that day he walked over and put a weighted vest on me. He never said a word, just came over and dropped about 20 pounds on my back. Wow. That vest pulled me down toward the ground, and suddenly I wasn't talking anymore—I was focusing on staying upright.

That was his way of teaching me to shut my trap and do the work. But it was great because he was genuinely concerned for us and wanted us to be ready for the jungles of Burma. One day he even appraised us and, in a moment of honesty, said he could have used more time before our trip to get us into proper shape but that he did the best he could. I think he did a pretty good job.

Honestly, though? Our training didn't come close to preparing us for our second trip to Burma.

PART THREE

Into Hard Places

*Trust in the L̜ORD with all your heart,
And lean not on your own understanding;
In all your ways acknowledge Him,
And He shall direct your paths.*

PROVERBS 3:5-6

6

A Bullet and the Heart of a Girl

April 2017

The road from Erbil to Mosul feels like a descent—not in elevation, but spiritually, emotionally. It's like swimming down into
deep water, farther down, farther down, and the pressure is building
on your ears and the water around you gets darker. I guess I feel this
way for many reasons: With every mile covered, we are getting closer
to a war zone; the farther we go, the more soldiers and checkpoints we
encounter. But we aren't headed for the front line of the war against
ISIS; we are headed for a trauma hospital built by Samaritan's Purse to
spend time with women and children impacted by terror. I am eager
to get there.

There are checkpoints along that road every 10 or 15 minutes, and at
each checkpoint our wonderful driver, Shocker, jokes with the guards
he knows (which seems to be most of them), acts professionally with
the ones he doesn't know, and gets us through in a fraction of the time
it would have taken us if we had come on our own. Once, when the
line to get through a particular checkpoint was backed up at least a
quarter mile, he drove into the lane of oncoming traffic, beeping his

horn, speeding to the front of the line. At first, the guards were upset with him, waving him to the side and shouting. But then they realized who it was. They started giving him a good-natured hard time. By the time they let us through, even the most serious guard was chuckling.

Usually this is because he tells the guards he is transporting ISIS. Everyone looks into the van, sees us, and seems to find this funny.

We go through one last, large checkpoint, weaving around traffic, driving on the shoulder. Then the road straightens and takes us into villages just east of Mosul. The farther we go, the more destruction we see. At first it seems like only random buildings have been destroyed, but as we get closer to the hospital, nearly every building is affected: Roofs are blown off, walls have caved in, and cratering caused by bullets pockmarks the surfaces.

The van slows down. It stops in the road. We wait as Shocker jumps out and goes over to a chain-link fence with a sliding gate. I watch him talk to some soldiers. They nod. He comes back into the van.

"We're here," he says, turning the van toward the gate. It opens in front of us.

There are a few different checkpoints on the way into the hospital grounds, and at each one we have to show our passports and they are checked against a list on a clipboard. Finally, we park. We are maybe 20 miles from the center of Mosul, where the fighting still goes on as the Iraqis try to finally expel ISIS from the city. Standing outside the tall cement walls of the hospital, I feel exposed. I look around. About 100 yards out from the hospital walls, a chain-link fence topped with razor wire surrounds the grounds. Just on the other side of the fence is a deep, wide ditch meant to keep any vehicles from driving through the chain link. Beyond that, there are grassy fields, relaxed and quiet in the breeze. Across the street is what looks like a suburban neighborhood, but I see no people, and nearly every building has experienced some degree of destruction.

"Come on, guys," the guide from our host NGO says, and we follow him through a metal door into the hospital.

I'm not supposed to tell you too much about the layout or the security features, for obvious reasons, but I can tell you that when we first walk in, it is quiet. There is a feeling of reverence, of peace, of people doing good work that leads to healing. It is a respite in a place recently overrun by violence and war. The ground is made up of crushed stones, and there is no ceiling—just the high concrete blast walls reaching up toward the low, gray sky. Our feet make crumbling sounds as we walk. There are trailers inside, accommodations for nurses and doctors and other staff. We meet a few people who work there, and they show us around.

We walk over to the entrance where ambulances drop off patients.

"For the first few weeks the hospital was here, we could hear mortars and gunfire all day long. And this area was always backed up. Sometimes five, ten ambulances were waiting just outside the walls to drop off their patients. Security had to check each patient to make sure they weren't carrying ordinance or weapons," one of the assistants who works there tells us. She smiles. "As you can see, things aren't so busy anymore. The battle is mostly in west Mosul, so we're seeing fewer trauma injuries here. We've actually started taking a few scheduled surgeries, since that seems to be the main need now."

There is some movement around the door as a new patient approaches so they show us to another part of the hospital. We walk into these very sturdy-looking tents, almost like solid pavilions, and find out that these are the operating rooms. If I wasn't inside a tent, I would think I was in an operating room in the United States. The equipment looks state-of-the-art. One of the doctors confirms this, saying the operating rooms in that makeshift hospital rival the operating rooms in the US city where he works. The doctors coming and going are dressed exactly as they would be in any US hospital. There is all manner of equipment lining the walls of the tent.

There's also an X-ray on the wall, as if it's been left there from when the previous patient had been examined. I wander over toward it, stare a little closer.

It looks like the image of a bullet inside a very small body.

"Yes," our guide says. "That little girl was hiding out in Mosul for three days after being shot. The bullet ricocheted and stopped so that the tip of the bullet is up against her heart. She just came in. We're trying to determine if we can take the bullet out here or if we should stabilize her and send her on to the hospital in Erbil."

We stand there, stunned, staring at the X-ray. The bullet is a sharp white against the black of her body cavity. Her ribs and backbone and pelvis are a kind of shaded gray.

There is a bullet inside a little girl, I tell myself. *A bullet up against her heart.*

It is almost too much to bear.

Later we eat lunch with some of the staff working at the hospital. They come from countries all around the world. I am amazed at these people who come from so far away to a dangerous place in order to help strangers stay alive.

Over one of their CBs I hear a security guard raise an alert.

"I'm seeing something in the air. Anyone else seeing it?"

Recently ISIS has been using drones to drop armed grenades on innocent people. I listen more intently to the conversation on the radio.

"Where are you seeing it? Over."

"Just beyond the road," the first voice says.

There is a long pause.

"That, my friends, is a balloon. Over."

The men on the radio chuckle. Even a floating balloon is enough to put the hospital on high alert.

Meanwhile, the girl in front of me is telling a story.

"Not too long ago there was a double car-bombing in the city. The ambulances brought the wounded and lined up all the way onto the road. There were dozens of people injured. We took people in as quickly as possible, but many of them were already dead or dying. Those people were taken into a separate area and placed on gurneys."

She pauses.

"Every single doctor and nurse was on duty. Even those who had been taking a break or were asleep. It was at night. One of the things we do here, with every single person who is dying, is we have someone sit with them, pray with them. We sing songs until they pass. But there were no medical staff left—they were all treating people. So I went into the room with all of the dying, along with some of my friends here, and we sang and prayed with them."

The ministry of presence.

We walk to the children's area and are first taken into the tent for little girls. There are 20 or so cots set up and a nurses' station. There are three or four nurses making the rounds. The little girls look up at us with wide eyes and a few bashful smiles. The mothers are protective but also welcoming, nodding their hellos.

I ask Murray if he will play the guitar while we spend some time with the little girls and their mothers. He plays "Jesus Loves Me" and "Jesus Loves the Little Children." He is an expert at that kind of thing, improvising in the moment. His voice covers the rest of us as we mingle with the mothers, and his singing has other people peeking inside the tent flaps, wondering what wonderful thing is happening in the children's tent.

I spend time with some of the girls. A few of the mothers speak English, but not many. Sometimes a translator will come over and help us communicate. But for the most part I am sitting beside someone I cannot talk to, smiling, trying to offer the encouragement of simply sitting beside them. These are mothers whose children have nearly been killed and little girls who have been through terrifying experiences. Sitting with them, not talking, at first it feels strange, but not for long.

There is a little girl whose mother I do not see. I go over and sit on a tiny chair beside her bed. She is sitting up and crying quietly, her legs stretching out straight and stiff under the sheet. I put my hand on her tiny shoulder, and she keeps crying. I call someone over.

"Is she okay?" I ask. I wonder, *Isn't there something we can be doing to help her?*

"This little girl's mother died in the same explosion that injured her," they told me. "She has been like this ever since she came out of surgery." I continue to sit with her, wait with her. It feels like such a small gesture in light of all she's been through.

We make our way to where the boys are treated in the neighboring tent. It is the same there, except it is mostly fathers and uncles and older brothers sitting alongside the beds. Two of the boys have large braces holding serious breaks in place. Most of the boys seem to have hand injuries: burns or breaks or amputations. They clap when Murray sings "This is the Day That the Lord Has Made," a few of them with both hands wrapped in gauze, patting their injured hands together and laughing.

"The force of a blast will often be so strong that it will break the hands or feet of a child, even if they are not hit by debris," I remember the security expert telling us in our initial briefing. "The shock wave alone can do that."

Beside me, a boy begins to moan. He pulls his blanket up over his head, arches his back, and lets out a long, low groaning that seems to emanate from his soul and have no end. I glance around, wondering why someone isn't helping him. He seems to be in a lot of pain. An older man goes over to the bed, but instead of consoling the boy or offering him some sympathy, the old man scolds him, shushes him. I look over at the nurse to try to figure out what is going on.

"He's autistic," she explains. "That's the boy's uncle. His father is recovering in the men's ward until he can be ID'd as not being with ISIS."

One of the girls who works in the hospital asks Murray for his guitar and sits down beside the autistic boy. She starts strumming chords, three or four different ones, creating a simple, steady melody that comes and goes like waves. The other boys in the room, the ones with both of their hands wrapped in bulbous bandages, clap gingerly in time with the strumming and smile. The boy beside me, the boy who had been moaning, peeks out from under the blanket. His dark eyes are unblinking. His mouth is closed and silent. And still she keeps playing, and he keeps watching her fingers dancing on the strings.

Then the little autistic boy starts to sing.

His voice is mystical, magical, in the way Arabic singing is. It's like the sound of a different era, like his voice is coming to us from a thousand years ago, through narrow city streets and over boulder-covered mountains. And remarkably, his singing is in perfect pitch, perfect rhythm. The girl continues strumming, and he keeps singing, the words wavering out to us.

Someone asks the interpreter what he is singing.

She smiles a sad smile.

"He is singing a lullaby to his mother," she says softly, tears welling up in her eyes. "His mother who is now dead."

Murray's refrain echoes in my soul.

Jesus, Jesus, Jesus.

Before we go, we ask about the little girl with the bullet against her heart.

"We think she's going to be fine," we're told. "She's been sent by ambulance to Erbil, and the bullet had not punctured the lining around her heart. They'll decide how to proceed when she arrives in the city."

We leave the hospital, going back out through the sliding chain-link gate, back out on to the quiet roads. We turn left and keep going closer to the city, then veer off the main road and follow winding streets through the suburbs. Nearly every house is destroyed. Nearly every wall is broken down.

The van pulls to a stop, and we get out.

It is eerie there in the middle of an empty city, so many houses destroyed and not a single person around. Then a car careens past us and turns a corner, disappearing in the maze of broken roads. A man drives up in a tractor with a scoop on it and begins tearing up the road. Shocker asks him what he and his friend are doing, why they are digging up the road. They answer, and he interprets for us.

"He says they are looking for the water main to fix it and try to get water back to this part of the city." He shrugs. There is no one else around. Not a single person.

"This is what I wanted to show you," our guide says, taking us across the street so that we can see the side of one of the buildings, a tall, flat surface that somehow the bombs did not find. There, spray-painted in black, is the ISIS flag. But this one is different, and that's when I notice there is also red spray-paint, lines of Arabic that have been painted on top of the ISIS flag.

"The black image," our guide says, "is the ISIS flag. But someone has come along since this area has been liberated and spray-painted something over it. The red writing in Arabic says something entirely different."

We look at him. I think he is enjoying the suspense.

"What does it say?" I finally ask.

"It says, 'Jesus is the light of the world.'"

7

The Long Trek

During the lead-up to our second trip to Burma, the trip when we would go on an impossible hike into the heart of the jungle, all the way to the village that serves as a base for the FBR mission, I became acutely aware, again, of the unlikely nature of God using someone like me to help children affected by terror. Who was I? What talents did I bring to the table? Why would God choose someone like me to accomplish this task?

"I'm more like Malibu Barbie than G.I. Jane," I said to Jen and Murray while we were hiking one day, and the image stuck in my mind. "Why has God chosen me to meet these incredible people?"

Murray, Jen, and I departed on our second trip to Burma in December of 2014. We were pumped. We had done all that training, worked our tails off in the gym, climbed the Albuquerque mountains, and it was finally time to make it happen. We were going to hike into Burma. We'd have to carry our own backpacks—anything we needed for that ten days, we had to take with us on our own shoulders.

Tied to my pack, partially as a way to lighten up the trip and partially as motivation, was a Barbie doll. Wherever I went, she went. If I slept in the dirt, she slept in the dirt. Having the doll was a joke, but it also ended up being a reminder to me that no matter how out-of-place

I felt, no matter what others might think of me being in the jungle, I was there for a reason. God had taken me there, exactly as I was, for a purpose.

We left for Burma with real hope. Our first trip to the Far East had at the beginning felt empty, or at least unfinished—none of the organizations we met fit into our specific vision of helping children impacted by terror. But then, at the end of the trip, we had met Dave Eubank, his family, and the Free Burma Rangers. Seeing what they did, hearing what they were up to, made us feel like we were getting closer. The Good Life Clubs they offered to children helped address their physical and spiritual needs. That was something we thought we'd like to be part of.

Were the Free Burma Rangers the right partner for us, for Reload Love? That's what we were hiking all the way into the jungle to find out.

We landed in Chiang Mai again, and this time I was not wearing my golden shoes. A driver took us to where Dave lived when he was in that city, which is really a kind of wood-hewn hut—more sophisticated than a hut, but with that general sort of feel. Jen, Murray, and I spent the night there, trying to pump ourselves up for the long trek into the jungle the following day.

I stared at the Barbie doll tied to my backpack, sleeping on the floor beside me. I thought of all the training the three of us had done to get ready for the trip. I thought of the miles and miles of wilderness we would have to hike through the following day. I slept lightly, my mind spinning with so many hopes and questions. And, if I'm honest, doubts. I wondered if I could really do it, if I could make this long hike into Burma.

Dave wasn't at his house in Chiang Mai—he was already in the jungle, living at his place in the village where the FBR trained the local people—so two of his guys met us at breakfast. All morning I was thinking about the two-day hike we'd have to manage, the only way to get to the village where FBR was based. Once again, that morning I was feeling nervous about my ability to make it so far into the jungle.

Most of the FBR guys are ex-military, or that's how it seemed to be, and one of our two guides, Adam, fit that description. The other guy's name was Jonathan. He had not served in the military, but he had achieved the fastest male climb of Mount Rainier. No big deal, right? This was the caliber of people I was about to hike with. I think he had also worked with Wycliffe Bible Translators at some point, and his job had involved hiking into secluded communities and building relationships with them.

Both men were sizing up the three of us and probably wondering how in the world we were going to make it in. Perhaps I got off on the wrong foot when I asked one of them, "Is your name Sherpa?"

"What do you mean?"

"I'm pretty sure you're going to have to Sherpa me in," I said, laughing. Of course, they played dumb.

I have to give them credit—no matter how much they might have doubted me at that point, they never once allowed their doubt to show.

We headed out. For the next six or seven hours, we sat in a truck that drove first on the city streets, then on country roads, then into a Thai national park, and finally onto dirt roads with huge divots and potholes. I couldn't sit there without bracing my core and holding on to something.

Adam, an ex-military guy, assigned to us by FBR, came with us on this trip, and he was somehow able to put his rucksack in front of him, lay down his head, and go right to sleep! But I couldn't relax like that. I was worried my head might fall off at the next huge bump.

At one point we met up with another Free Burma Ranger named Eliya. Dave nicknamed him the pirate angel, and he's a huge figure in this story. Dave and Eliya first met in the early days of Dave's work in Thailand, when the Karen people were pouring over the border, fleeing persecution in Burma. Dave loaded up a truck with some medical supplies and headed into the middle of this mass of hurting, running, broken humanity.

As Dave was wondering how he could possibly treat all these wounded people, a man came out of the jungle. It was Eliya.

"Who are you?" Dave asked.

"I am the last medic," Eliya said calmly, and he joined Dave, helping wherever he could. They would come up on groups of injured people and triage them, treat the ones they could, and send the others farther along. They got to the last person, a man whose leg had been damaged horribly by a landmine. They put a tourniquet on it and carried the man out. When they finally arrived at Dave's truck, Eliya said, "Okay. See you later."

"Where are you going?" Dave asked.

"I have to go find my family."

"You have family?" Dave asked, incredulous.

"Yes, we were all fleeing through this region," Eliya said.

"Why would you leave them behind?"

"One, I have good friends who take care of my family. Two, I am the last medic."

He left, found his family, and later rejoined Dave as a member of the Free Burma Rangers.

> If you want to be my disciple, you must, by comparison, hate everyone else—your father and mother, wife and children, brothers and sisters—yes, even your own life. Otherwise, you cannot be my disciple (Luke 14:26 NLT).

At some point during the bouncing and twisting and turning, we stopped for food, and the meal ended up being a length of bamboo filled with sticky rice and beans and some kind of meat. You pull everything out of the bamboo and eat with your fingers. That was our boxed lunch. That was our paper bag.

As we got to know our guides better, we started joking with them.

"C'mon," I said. "There's got to be another way into the camp besides hiking, right? Airplane maybe? Speed boat?"

They laughed. I think they were finally getting used to us and our ways.

"But there really are no roads in?"

"None," one of them said.

"What if someone gets hurt? What if someone needs a doctor?"

He shrugged.

"The doctor hikes in or we carry you out."

We drove and we drove and we drove and the morning turned to afternoon. The jungle we traveled through was thick and green and full of shadows, and the vehicle continued lurching up and down. I hoped the paths we had to hike on were good paths. I hoped they were clearer than what I was looking at there on the Thailand side of the border. The jungle along the road looked impenetrable.

The vehicle stopped. I looked through the windows. We were parked beside a sandy area along the river.

"When we get on the beach," our driver said, "we'll throw your stuff out of the van and onto the sand. You'll need to grab your backpack, run down to the shoreline as fast as possible, and get into the boat that will be waiting."

He paused. I could hear my heart beating.

"This is a non-permissive crossing."

He stared at me.

"You'll need to be under the tarp," he said, pointing at my head. "Blonde hair. You'll draw too much attention if someone does spot us."

I nodded. What had I gotten myself into?

"Once you're on the boat, stay low. Someone will throw your stuff onto the beach when you get to the other side. At that point you need to grab it and run for cover. Fast. If the Burmese border patrol sees you, they'll revoke your passport and send you home."

Did I mention the backpack weighed 50 pounds?

"Everyone ready?" he asked. We nodded our heads. They drove onto the sand and threw out our things. We hopped out, grabbed our backpacks, and ran for the boat. Then we were in the boat, and I was hunched over, trying to stay under the tarp. The outboard motor fought against the water, and waves slapped the bottom of the boat as we took off for the Burmese side of the river. Everything was loud and chaotic and jarring.

It was a quick ride, maybe 15 minutes, and soon I felt the boat slowing down. I peeked out from under the tarp. I saw the thick jungle approaching, then felt the boat bump up against the bank. Again, they tossed our things into the sand. Barbie, still clinging to the side of the backpack, fell face-first into the ground. We grabbed our bags and ran as fast as we could through the sand, our feet slipping and sliding beneath us.

We vanished into the jungle.

After a long day on the road, a bouncy, never-ending journey on the truck, and a quick sprint up the beach, I felt emotionally ready for the challenging hike to come. I was prepared. We were about to hike through the jungles of Burma, and I could do it.

The sun was getting low in the sky, and it was already dark there, under the trees. That's when I heard the sound of a loud, persistent motor approaching. I looked at the guys and they looked at us, shrugging their shoulders. I'm not sure if they even knew what was going on at that point.

I saw the tractor. Somehow Dave had found a guy willing to let us borrow his tractor for the trek into the jungle. *This will work,* I thought to myself. One of the Free Burma Rangers, who went by the name Monkey, drove it out to pick us up. Now we were traveling with both Eliya and Monkey, two of FBR's most trusted guys and perhaps Dave's top two men. Of course, you'd never know this by the way they carried themselves—they were as meek and unassuming as anyone I've ever met. The fact that Dave sent them out to meet up with and escort us newbies was a huge honor.

Eliya, the one who joined us on the Thai side of the river, was jocular. He loved to laugh and play his guitar. I came to think of him as FBR's head medic, although I'm not sure he has that official title.

Monkey, on the other hand, was meek and quiet. He's the kind of person everyone listens to when he has something to say. When he did speak, he usually said something godly, something faith-based and important. He seemed to be the head of FBR's chaplains.

We started tying all of our backpacks on to the metal beast in the half-light. Murray, Adam, Jonathan, and Monkey climbed onto the back and found places to hold on. The front of the tractor was missing the scoop, but it still had the lifting apparatus, so they created a rough seat out of some boards and told Jen and me we could sit at the front. There was a bar going across, so we sat on the wooden boards and let our legs dangle down under the bar, which we could also use to hang on, and then they belted us into place with some ropes. If this sounds like an extremely precarious position, then you understand the situation—if the tractor tipped forward, there was no way we could scramble out of that spot in time. If that happened, we would probably break or lose our legs. I squeezed Jen's hand in a death grip, and we looked at each other with wide eyes. In case you haven't picked up on it, we exchanged that look of disbelief a lot during this trip. The tractor gathered itself, the engine roared, and we were off.

After the first few hundred yards, I seriously considered turning down the tractor offer, untying myself from that death trap, and hiking on foot. We had barely driven away from the river when the trail started going up a steep hill. I felt like the tractor might tip over backward at any point. About the time Jen and I started to get a handle on the uphill climb, we hit the top and started back down, the tractor descending on the hairpin turns of the trail. Then it felt like the whole thing would roll forward, end over end.

At one point, after it was nearly dark and the only light was coming from our flashlights, the tractor started tipping back, and everyone shouted, and the men jumped off the back, and the tractor thudded back onto all its wheels. Not long after that, the wheels slipped and slid, spun sideways, and we collided hard with the muddy side of the mountain. The tires spun in the muck. The darkness pressed in around us.

This entire time Jen and I were dangling from the front.

The view that night is almost impossible to describe, but I'll try. The path, barely wide enough for the tractor, wound its way up and down. It inched along ravines that, because it was dark, we couldn't see to the bottom of. If we slid down into one of those, we would have died. The jungle closed in around us with all of its sounds and earthy smells, low branches, and encroaching plants. The sky above us, when we could see it through the trees, was a patchwork of stars.

Of course, the guys all thought the trip on the tractor was hysterical and adventurous. Especially when I took out my Barbie doll and tied her to the front in between Jen and me. But there we were, this small team of people on a trek deep into Burma, riding a moaning tractor, slipping and sliding our way into the middle of nowhere.

Normally, if you're going in by foot (which is the only way the Free

Burma Rangers ever do it), you stop halfway and spend the night, but since we were driving on the tractor, they decided to drive straight through. What a day that was, waking up in the morning in Thailand, going on the long drive, taking the boat across the rough river, and then being strapped onto a tractor. All on day one.

I was exhausted. Even on the lurching, slipping tractor, I had trouble keeping my eyes open. It was getting close to midnight, and I started seeing fires in the jungle.

"What are those fires?" I called back to one of our guides, shouting over the noise of the tractor.

"That's where shepherds are camping," one of the men said. "They've stopped for the night with their sheep."

I stared off into the darkness, the tractor rumbling on, and for a moment it felt like I was traveling to a place no other human had ever been before, somewhere on the edge of the universe.

The tractor pulled into a village and stopped. When the driver turned off the ignition, a silence rushed in like I have never heard before. I could literally feel the quiet.

"Is this it? Are we there?" I asked. It seemed too good to be true.

It was.

"We still have about two hours of hiking," Monkey said. "But the tractor stays here."

They untied our things and threw them down. I pulled out my headlamp and put it on, the light shining out in front of me. I hefted my backpack up onto my shoulders. We were on the final leg of our journey.

I felt like a zombie during that last stretch into the village. I expected we'd at least be hiking on a path and was unprepared for all the wet and slippery logs we had to walk along or the amount of jumping we had to do from rock to rock. When the rocks were too far apart, we tightrope walked along strips of bamboo someone had strapped together long ago. I tried not to look down into the deep shadows beneath me.

At the very end we came to these large rice paddies, and the only way across those was along bamboo bridges. Everything was covered in that late-night mist, and it was so dark, and we were all exhausted.

There, the bamboo was slick, and my feet threatened to slip out from under me.

Finally, we arrived at the village of Per Der Ler, the base for the Free Burma Rangers.

It was so late when we got there—I have no idea exactly what the time was, but it felt to me like we had entered some kind of never-ending night. We entered the village and walked into an area where there were three or four huts in a circle with some picnic tables in the middle, again made out of bamboo.

"Hey!" a voice shouted, and we turned around, and in the bobbing light of all those head lamps I recognized Dave Eubank coming toward us.

"Oh, Dave," I said, so happy to see him, and even I was surprised at how tired my voice sounded. There was a small fire. Dave had a head-lamp on too, so I couldn't look directly at his face. All the moving and bobbing lights disoriented me. It was like we were all standing in a circle of light, and everything beyond us was only darkness in every direction. What a strange, strange experience.

Even though it was late, they had some food for us, and we sat at the tables and ate. Rice, probably, although I can't remember for sure. Dave was talking, but his voice was in the background of my mind as I began to comprehend how deep into the nothingness we were.

There is no easy way out of here, I thought as I ate and listened to Dave and felt the quiet of the jungle. *There's no helicopter coming to get me if I get hurt, no ambulance to drive me to a hospital. If I need to get out of here, if I need to get home, I have to walk out on my own two feet. There isn't even a tractor anymore! That thing is long gone.*

Dave told us how the village had been ransacked and burned down five times by the Burmese army. Five! He pointed out the small church and gave us the lay of the land while we sleepily swallowed the rice.

"Everything should be fine while you're here," he said in his matter-of-fact voice. "The Burmese army isn't advancing right now. But still, keep your shoes close at all times. Keep your backpacks close and ready. You know that rice paddy you came through?"

Jen and I nodded, our headlamps bobbing up and down.

"Well," he continued, "if something goes sideways, run there and meet us at the river."

Wait, what? He thinks I know where I am?

I looked out into the darkness. I couldn't even remember from which direction we had entered the clearing.

"You think I could run back there?" I asked him, disbelief in my voice.

"By the river," he said again, nodding. "If something goes wrong, meet us by the river."

Jen and I looked at each other.

Oh my.

Someone led Jen and me up a ladder and into a bamboo hut. There was a fire pit in the middle for warmth and for cooking. I laid down on the hard floor, inside my sleeping bag, and could feel a small amount of warmth radiating out of the ashes. Not too long ago there must have been a fire there. Jen laid down on the other side, and that was how we bunked for the night. I immediately fell into a fitful sleep.

As the hours crept by, it got colder and colder. I don't know who found who, but at some point Jen and I moved around the fire so that we could be closer together and find some warmth. It just kept getting colder as the night progressed!

Early in the morning someone came into the hut and lit a fire for us, an act I'm sure was meant to be helpful, but also served as a way of smoking us out of our hut and making sure we started our day on time. We emerged coughing, eyes watering. Jen and I walked fifty yards or so to a hut that served as an outhouse. Later we were given water that had been boiled and sat down for breakfast at the picnic table.

The Eubanks' kids have a few horses there that they were taking care of and riding around on. They galloped back and forth. Sahalee, Dave's oldest daughter, was holding a monkey. These kids understood jungle and tribal life in ways I couldn't even imagine. They seemed so at ease in their surroundings, with nothing to fear. I thought that if things did "go sideways," in Dave's words, I would gladly follow one of his children into the jungle. I had no doubt they would keep me safe.

We brought our own cup and spoon to the bamboo table, and when breakfast was ready they brought out plates and put the food in the middle. You had to be ready to grab whatever they gave you. I was hungry, so whatever they served was fine by me.

After we finished breakfast, I started walking around the camp, and when I came around a corner, the view took my breath away. I walked to the edge of the rice paddy, stared out at the surrounding jungle shrouded in mist, and couldn't believe I was there. It was so quiet, even at the edge of the village, that I could hear the morning dew dropping off the palm trees. It was the time of year that they burned off the rice paddies in preparation for the following season, and the smoke simmered up, hiding the morning sun. The paddies themselves were laid out in large squares, and people walked the edges of the squares on their way to here and there. I was stunned by the beauty of that Burmese morning.

And I was also afraid.

That was one of the few times, maybe even the only time, in all of my travels when I felt afraid. It was a panicky feeling, a kind of suffocation that there was no way out. I was as far off the grid as a person could be. I didn't have a phone. I couldn't drive anywhere. If something happened to me, if there was an accident or I became deathly ill, someone would have to carry me out.

"Excuse me?" someone said. "But are you Lenya Heitzig?"

I turned and found a handsome, broad-shouldered gentleman staring at me in surprise.

"Uh, yes," I said, taken aback.

"*The* Lenya Heitzig?"

I nodded.

"The wife of Skip Heitzig?"

I nodded again, this time laughing.

"Yes to all of those," I said. "And who are you?"

"I'm Victor Marx," he said, and I couldn't believe it. Victor is a humanitarian, a child and youth advocate who speaks all around the world on behalf of abused children. It turned out he was traveling with Greg Birch, a silver-star Army Ranger. Someone said of Birch: "If Captain America had a hero, this guy would be it."[3]

And there, in the jungle with men like Victor Marx and Greg Birch, was me, Lenya Heitzig.

"What in the world are you doing here?" Victor asked me. "The Burmese army is only a few miles away." There was concern in his voice.

I'll be honest, hearing that, and suddenly realizing I was in a place usually reserved for Special Forces, increased my feeling of insecurity.

Lord, what am *I doing here?*

On that first morning I was still so tired I almost cried. It was a bone weariness, an exhaustion I had never felt before. Standing there, staring out across the rice paddies, I considered the hike back out, wondering how in the world I would ever do it. I realized how ill-equipped I was to make that trek again, this time without the aid of a tractor. It was a drowning feeling, like I was barely treading water and about to drop below the surface.

But then I started praying. And I kept looking out at the beauty around me.

Lord, why did You bring me here? What are You trying to show me? This can't be about my weakness or my fears. I know You didn't bring me here to make me feel afraid. What do You want to show me?

Again, I heard Him say very clearly, *Lenya, I have been faithful to every generation.*

And in the quiet, I heard Him say something else. *Lenya, I have even been faithful to you.*

I took out my Bible and started reading Psalm 119:89-96:

> Forever, O LORD,
> Your word is settled in heaven.
> Your faithfulness endures to all generations;
> You established the earth, and it abides.
> They continue this day according to Your ordinances,
> For all are Your servants.
> Unless Your law had been my delight,
> I would then have perished in my affliction.
> I will never forget Your precepts,
> For by them You have given me life.

I am Yours, save me;
For I have sought Your precepts.
The wicked wait for me to destroy me,
But I will consider Your testimonies.
I have seen the consummation of all perfection,
But Your commandment is exceedingly broad.

Your faithfulness endures to all generations. You established the earth, and it abides. What an amazing promise.

Okay, God, I thought taking a deep breath and regrouping. *I'm in. We can do this.*

I started meditating on that, on His faithfulness, on how He has always been there for me, for the people I know, for the Karen tribe. Jen came over to where I was standing, I told her how I felt, and we started praying together. We walked back to the hut and prayed some more, casting off the fear I was feeling, determined to trust Him with the entire week. I was not going to let any fear or darkness keep me from seeing and learning the things He had brought us so far to see and learn.

Later that first morning Dave came out to where we were sitting and showed us pictures of Hugh Seagram, the man who had come into the jungle during World War II, and his Burmese counterpart, Deegay Tu. The latter held two machetes—apparently he was a deadly warrior, wielding the long knives like lawn mower blades, and he had been the leader of Tha Dah Der in those days. I thought again about the words he first spoke to Seagram when Seagram made his way into the Burmese jungles.

"If you're with God, we're with you. If you're not with God, we're not with you."

"When I came into the jungle, I heard the same thing," Dave said. "They would tell me that if I was with God, they were with me, and if I was not with God, they were not with me. That's a humbling thing, answering that question. 'Are you with God?'"

So Dave picked up the training and continued helping the Karen tribe protect themselves.

"Today," Dave told us, "there is a memorial service being held for a grandfather who served with Seagram. His name is Mawa. We're going to go to his village, meet his wife, and pay homage to this man and his service to the Karen people."

We left our compound and hiked through the jungle. The paths we followed wound up and over hills and along ravines. I remember thinking, *I thought I was here to see if FBR is a good fit for Reload Love, but here I am, taking part in their history.* As we walked, Dave's children blazed past us, back and forth, riding horses and carrying Karen flags.

We arrived at the edge of the village and entered a large, square hut with a pitched roof that came down low at the back of the house. We all sat down on the floor and ate the food they had prepared for us: snacks and tea and a kind of sugar candy that tasted like caramel. It was dark inside those dense bamboo walls.

Sitting there in the midst of all the people was Mawa's wife, Pipi, a diminutive older Karen woman. She was hunched over and dressed in tribal clothing that included a long skirt. She sat in the seat of honor, and in front of her was a makeshift stage where people began telling these legendary stories about her husband.

We listened as people shared about this man, and his wife sat there quietly the entire time, nodding her head, smiling at the memories. She seemed like such a humble woman. The man's grandson was even there—his nickname was Taxi because he served with the Free Burma Rangers and met people at the border, bringing them into the village.

Dave stood up and said some incredible words and then gave a medal to the man's wife, honoring Mawa's legacy. Before I knew it, Dave turned to me.

"You should say something," he said. "Go ahead."

"Me?" I asked.

He was always putting me on the spot like that. But besides that, I wondered why I would have the honor of speaking at such an important, intimate gathering. All of these people knew this man. I had never met him. I had never even heard of him until that day.

I stood up. The translator stared intently at me as I got my thoughts together.

"Thank you for letting me be here to see that God is in the jungle,"

I said. "I thought I was coming to a God-forsaken part of the world, but you Christians far surpass me in faith and have done more than I could imagine. I have never had to run for my life. I have never had to rebuild my church three times."

I wept while I spoke. The emotion of seeing God's tangible faithfulness to a group of people I had never even heard of was so moving.

"I am overwhelmed with God's love for you," I continued. "I'm overwhelmed with the providence of God, that He sees you, that He sent Adoniram Judson 200 years ago, that He sent Seagram 70 years ago, that He sent Dave's father 50 years ago, that He sent Dave 25 years ago. I'm overwhelmed at how God is faithful to each and every generation."

I looked around, amazed that I could be part of such a rich history. *God,* I asked again, *why am I here? What do You want to do with Reload Love?*

We walked down to the grandfather's gravesite, and some of the young men helped Pipi make that short hike. The grave was surrounded by bamboo and covered with flowers and other things they had placed there. We sang a few worship songs. It was such a beautiful moment.

Dave kept us busy for the next few days. The day after the funeral we visited the church that had been burned down three times by the Burmese army. It was close to Christmastime, so they had a Christmas tree inside their bamboo, thatched-roof church. It was decorated with balloons! What a whimsical service. They asked us if we would participate so we went up with Murray and sang a song.

The day after that we did a Good Life Program with the Free Burma Rangers. All the kids came in from the surrounding villages far and wide. This meant every single person in Tha Dah Der was busy. The place was like a disturbed ant hill. They were making food and preparing the medical clinic to train doctors and nurses. They asked us to make a big sign and to help count out the packs for the kids that included toothbrushes and other toiletry items.

On the day the Good Life Program began, we started early. Karen, Dave's wife, was an incredible leader—she got the kids moving with an extensive calisthenics program. This was crucial in getting all the wiggles out of the kids. Then they ran a 5K race around the rice paddies. Someone asked me if I wanted to run, but seeing as I had barely made it into the village, I thought I'd sit it out. Of course Jen ran, and she did fantastic.

The leaders did a skit (I think it was of the good Samaritan), sang some songs, and by then it was time to break for lunch. I was taking photos and watching them run the program and checking out the medical clinic, where they were not only treating children but also training medics from other villages. There were hundreds of kids around, all of these beautiful, colorful children.

This went on all day. At night the children went up to the church building to watch the Superbook cartoon.

That night, when they were up at the church, I stood back in amazement. This was what our Reload Love money could support: incredible programs like these that made a tangible difference in the lives of children impacted by terror. Of course, part of me also looked out into the shadows and wondered how in the world I had ended up there, in the middle of the Burmese jungle.

The trip was changing me in so many ways. It would take me a long time to process. But the trip was also about to have a big impact on the direction of Reload Love.

8

The Black Banner

During our final days in Burma, there was a night meeting of the Free Burma Rangers. Dave invited our team to sit in on it, and once again I was honored. Who was I to be giving feedback to them? Who was I to be included in their plans?

I went to the meeting, and all the tribal leaders who had been training with Dave that week were there. So many tribes. So many ethnicities and religions and hopes represented.

It turned out, Dave's heart was in Iraq. He was seeing the children there, the ones impacted by ISIS and terror and war, and he wanted to help. But when you're Dave Eubank, how do you decide where and when to allocate your limited resources? Why Iraq, when there were so many other hurting people in the world?

"What do you think?" Dave suddenly asked me, and for a moment I felt like a deer in headlights. At Reload Love, we had been thinking and praying for the people in Iraq, believing on behalf of the entire region that the black banners of ISIS would be brought down. I had been devastated by the events that had taken place in Sinjar and on the Sinjar Mountains where the Yazidis had fled, and the images of starving children on the top of the mountain were fresh in my mind. We wanted to help people in Iraq.

"Well, when it comes to our church in Albuquerque," I said, "Skip always leads with Acts 1:8 in mind: 'You shall receive power when the Holy Spirit has come upon you; and you shall be witnesses to Me in Jerusalem, and in all Judea and Samaria, and to the end of the earth.' So we started in Jerusalem, which for us was Albuquerque, before moving to Judea and Samaria, or the southwest of the US. After that, foreign missions were the end of the earth."

I paused, looking around the circle. There was so much wisdom in that group, so much desire to do the thing God was calling them to do.

"Maybe for you, Tha Da Der is Jerusalem, and Burma is Judea and Samaria. Maybe it's time for you to move to the ends of the earth. Maybe Iraq is the next place God is preparing you to go."

Dave was nodding. I could tell he was seriously considering what I had said.

"The other thing I'm thinking," I said, continuing, "is that you all have a knowledge of living tribally that would serve you well in Iraq. Westerners like me don't understand tribal life, how tribes interact, what they're concerned with."

I gestured at all the men in the meeting.

"But all of you, you know tribal. You speak tribal. If Westerners go to Iraq, the Iraqis already have them labeled, but they won't know what to do with you brown brothers, especially when they see that you understand the way of the tribe. I think you should go to Iraq."

I paused.

"And if you go there," I said, "we want to go too."

At two o'clock the next morning, we woke up, got our things together, and prepared to make the two-day hike out, back to civilization. Our first day's hike would be to the Per Ler Der region, and the second day would take us all the way back to the river crossing. I had been dreading this hike the entire trip, ever since we drove in on a tractor. There would be no tractor this time around.

What I feared had come upon me.

A huge group was leaving that morning, so despite the early hour, the camp was bustling. There were men in army fatigues and tribal gear, and Dave was leading everyone. It felt like a big moment, with so many people departing. We were standing around in the cool, damp night, our heavy backpacks on, and Dave said a few things to the group, praising the teams who had been there.

"Before you go," Dave shouted, "I think we need to make sure we're warmed up. Let's do 25 jumping jacks and 100 push-ups!"

Seriously? I thought. *We've got this hike ahead of us and you're going to make us jump around?*

But I didn't wimp out. I did everything.

After the exercises, we all turned our headlamps on and started walking, one group at a time, out of camp along the path. We were like the seven dwarfs heading off to the mine. "Hi-ho, hi-ho! It's off to work we go!" Dave had designated two guides for us: Jonathan and Adam. Everyone else would eventually be peeling off, going in their own directions.

Dave sent off the Reload Love team in the first wave of hikers. It was cool, and mist hovered around the palms. The light from our headlamps shone on the fog. We hiked across the rice paddies on slick bamboo walkways. Jonathan was my closest support, showing me how to place my feet across the bamboo instead of in line with it. He stayed beside me, making sure I was okay.

The path followed a river bed, crossing over short bamboo bridges, and always went up, up, up. At some point, when it felt like we had reached a high elevation, Jonathan stopped.

"Look back," he said with a smile on his face. So I stopped hiking and turned around.

For as far as I could see, a line of lights was moving through the predawn jungle—these were the headlamps of everyone leaving Tha Dah Der, winding along the path, illuminating the darkness. It was like a moving line of stars. It was so beautiful, and I remember a song my musicianary friend Angela DiPrima wrote about the faith journey, using words from a poem from L.B.E. Cowan about those who go ahead of us and look back to cheer us on in our faith journey.

All of a sudden I felt like I was in *Pilgrim's Progress* and these were the lines of pilgrims on their way to the city. These beacons of light just kept moving, kept undulating, and I started crying. Jonathan was a theology student, and he started talking about Bible verses along the lines of God's faithfulness and the light that cannot be put out.

God's faithfulness.

Seeing those lights was like seeing a tangible time line of all that God had done in Burma through the centuries. Adoniram Judson. Hugh Seagram. The Eubank family. And there I was, blessed beyond measure to witness that point in time everything else had led to.

It took us an hour or two to get to a village with real roads. I felt good. It was rough going, but I had gone into it with a strong mind, determined to do this hard thing. But a surprise waited for us up on the road: The tractor was there!

"Are you serious?" I asked, laughing, and Jen and I resumed our position on the front of the metal beast. It took us from 2:00 a.m. until early in the afternoon to get to the village of Pa Da Der. We slept there that night in a house on stilts with the horses and mules underneath us. They were a troublesome bunch of animals, and I heard them fighting with each other throughout the night.

The next morning we woke up early, and we didn't have the tractor for that last day. We left once again while it was still dark, and it was time to split off from the Eubank crew, so Dave said a beautiful prayer for us and we parted ways. It hit me then that we were leaving, and I wondered if I would ever see them again. I thought I would. I thought we had found a wonderful group of people for Reload Love to partner with, but you never know how things will go.

There was no breakfast that morning, not even any coffee, so we drank piping-hot water and made our way on scarce supplies. It was misty in the jungle again, and we were going up very steep inclines. We'd crest one only to find there was another, larger peak to climb (after descending down into the valley). Jen is a gazelle, so we were moving at a good clip. By the time we made it to the final downhill that led to the river, my quads were shaking and threatening to cramp. My body was finished! We hadn't eaten all day, and it was after noon. I was glad to hear the river wasn't far off.

Then a huge surprise! Dave popped out of the jungle. I think he ran up ahead of us just to see if we could do it. I think he likes to see if people can do more than they think they can do, and he seemed pleased to see us there.

"Dave!" I said. I couldn't believe it was him.

We heard the hum of an outboard motor and moved toward the river. Before I knew it, we were saying another quick good-bye to Dave and jumping back on board the boat, heading back to where we had started the journey. I was under the tarp, and the boat was chopping through the waves to the Thailand side of the river. When we arrived we scrambled out, and in that moment one of our guides saw another boat coming.

Thai border guards? Burmese soldiers? We didn't know.

"Run for it!" someone shouted, and we climbed out onto the sand dune. The jungle forest was a few hundred yards away, and my backpack was heavy, and the dune we ran up was steep. I didn't think I would make it up, but someone else from our group grabbed me by the backpack and basically carried me to the top, the way you might carry a small cat by the scruff of the neck.

"Hit the dirt!" someone shouted, so we all fell flat on our faces and waited for the other boat to pass.

Eventually our truck came. Eventually we made it home.

But I was a different person. I felt like I was becoming more and more of a Free Burma Ranger. I wasn't making decisions based on fear or comfort or pride anymore. All of those things—fear, comfort, pride—got killed piece by piece in the jungle, and by the time I left, I felt like Malibu Barbie had completely transformed into G.I. Jane. It was a deep, foundational shift within me as a human being, something that needed to happen if I was to fulfill my purpose in the coming years.

I had also become more entrenched with tribal people. I felt closer to them after one week than I did with some people in my neighborhood, people I've lived beside for years! There was a camaraderie there in the huts that I loved, and these new friends were the ones who helped me navigate beyond my fear, my desire for comfort, and my pride. They pushed me. This is what the tribal life can do for you. I felt very small, in a good way, compared to the giants of the faith I was living with and hearing stories about.

Most of all I wanted to tell everyone what I had seen. I wanted to encourage people, to explain to our sleeping culture that there is something we can do to help the plight of terrorized children. I felt like if I didn't share my experiences, I might explode.

When I came home from that second Burma trip, I was excited. Things were moving, we were working together with FBR to support their work in Burma, and the Reload Love team as a whole was focusing and praying about what we might be able to do in Iraq. There was a tangible excitement in the air when we met. Our trip to Burma proved to each of us that we were on the right track and that God was willing to use us, even in the farthest, hardest places on earth.

One day a migraine put me on my back. I was at home, lying in bed, and that's when I pray the hardest, when I am in physical pain like that. But I've learned not just to pray for myself, for my own relief—so that day I also prayed that God might use that migraine as a way of pointing me toward something I might otherwise have missed in the busyness of my normal life.

Lord, what principality are we facing? I asked. *As we prepare to go to the Middle East, what are we up against? What is this darkness? Please show me.*

And God reminded me of the Bamboo Curtain that had been in place in China for so long, a geopolitical barrier that kept China separated from the rest of the world. Communism was certainly part of it, and it became illegal for Christians to worship or read the Bible. I knew people at the time who had smuggled Bibles through the Bamboo Curtain at great danger to themselves and those they worked with. But then the Bamboo Curtain fell, and now we are more free to share the gospel.

From there, God brought to my mind the Iron Curtain, also a geographical, political, and religious barrier. I remembered, when I was younger, hearing stories of missionaries who had snuck their way into the USSR and Eastern European countries for the sake of sharing the gospel. Christians had broken through that barrier.

I started trying to frame this Middle Eastern context in my mind. How did this compare to those curtains? The curtain there was also geographical, political, and religious.

What is the name of this curtain? I asked God, and there in my bed, in the middle of my migraine, God answered me.

It was the Black Curtain.

I had been diving into books about ISIS and Iraq, and they had all spoken about the importance of the black banners. These flags had been mentioned in some of Islam's religious and holy books, so groups like al-Qaeda and then ISIS had operated under them, knowing that when Muslims saw the black banners, they would recognize the religious significance. One of their holy books, the Hadith, said, "If you see black banners coming from Khurasan, join that army, even if you have to crawl over ice; no power will be able to stop them" and "They will finally reach Baitul Maqdis [Jerusalem] where they will erect their flags."[4] This is why al-Qaeda grew their hair and beards long. The black flags were their rallying cry.

I suddenly felt a deep understanding as to why the enemy was doing what it did. All of these books and passages and new revelations flooded my mind as I lay there with a migraine, and that's when God spoke again.

You need to pray against the black flags. Just like people have broken through the Bamboo Curtain and the Iron Curtain, you need to pray that the Black Curtain of ISIS flags comes down.

The next day I told the team at the office what I had read, what I had heard from God.

"Wouldn't it be lovely," I asked, "if anywhere a black banner has flown, we could leave our own banner declaring Jesus and His love? After all, when the king is in residence, they put up a banner. Our little banners, instead of encouraging hate, could encourage love."

That very same day one of the pastors at our church, a very prophetic man, was in the meeting with us. He had brought a scripture he had read that week to share with us, even before he heard what I had been thinking: "We will rejoice in your salvation, and in the name of our God we will set up our banners! May the LORD fulfill all your petitions" (Psalm 20:5).

God had spoken to two of us about the same thing! We started praying hard against the black banners of ISIS, pleading with God that

His banner of love would unfurl over the Middle East. That became our focus.

About this time we brought on someone to help us with our website and social media efforts. His name was Nick. He was a talented guy behind the camera and had experienced a lot of success in the YouTube world.

One of his first ideas for us was doing a money bomb. It's something people do to raise a lot of money in a short period of time. Basically, you designate a day or two, or maybe a weekend, set a monetary goal, and do a huge social media push during that time to try and hit your goal. The website is set up so that it looks like a bomb tick-tick-ticking until you hit the goal.

"Let's do it," I said, "but let's call it a love bomb."

Everyone was on board. We decided that whatever was raised would go with Skip on his upcoming trip to the Middle East. He would represent Reload Love over there for the first time, and one of his primary missions was to look for groups we could partner up with and help. So we chose a weekend to do the love bomb and then tried to come up with the amount of money we'd attempt to raise.

"Let's set a ridiculous goal," we decided. "Let's go for $45,000!"

We thought that was an audacious goal, well beyond our wildest dreams.

Nick set up the website, and it had this image of a thermometer filling up. Skip announced it at all the services, and we even passed the offering plate, something we rarely do. We had kiosks around the church campus, and the people collecting donations wore army helmets with hearts on them.

"Help us drop a love bomb!"

After the first service, we went over $45,000.

At one point I came on stage and said, "Let's go for $60,000!"

We went on to raise $145,000 that weekend! We had never tried to raise money before! It was such an incredible thing, and the Love Bomb became a Valentine's Day tradition for us.

Skip headed to Iraq, and he took all $145,000 with him. We didn't keep any of it for administration costs. He toured around, met various leaders of NGOs, and distributed the money. This was when he first toured Khanke Camp, the IDP camp that was a sea of white tents. The leads he generated during that trip would set the direction for us in the years to come.

As we focused more and more on Iraq, I started to see what other NGOs were doing. A lot of groups were using Iraq as a kind of PR experiment, and they were starting to look like dog-and-pony shows. Iraq had become the high-value place to show people you were working if you wanted to raise money. It was a notch in the belt.

I disdained that. I didn't want Reload Love to be that. I didn't want to be the organization that gave a token to Iraq in order to up donations and then evacuated without leaving something tangible, something of value.

"We have to be tangible," I insisted to my team. "We have to leave something behind—not just knick-knacks." I knew we had the resources to help with temporary things, but that didn't feel like enough.

That's when I thought, *We should build playgrounds.*

As I mentioned earlier, we had already helped build a playground at one of the NGOs we had met with in Cambodia, and it was a huge hit among the orphaned children. It felt like something they appreciated. I wondered if we could do something similar in Iraq for children impacted by ISIS.

I still remember the meeting I was in when I first floated the playground idea. There were a few other organizations there, and they had just started doing work in Iraq. These felt like bigger players to me, certainly more established organizations than Reload Love. But we had just begun thinking through this idea of turning battlegrounds into playgrounds, so I mentioned it there, in the meeting.

"At Reload Love," I said, "we've been thinking of investing in Iraq by building playgrounds in strategic locations." I glanced around to see what the reaction would be.

The idea fell on deaf ears.

One of the other leaders in the room shrugged off the idea. They weren't unkind, but they were definitely dismissive. I felt deflated. Maybe I wasn't thinking this through?

But as the meeting ended and everyone moved to a new location, a young man by the name of Nic McKinley turned to me. I didn't know Nic well at the time, but I would get to know him very well in the coming months. Later, when I found out what he did for a living and what kind of experience he had, I came up with a new name for him: Jason Bourne.

"The playground idea?" Nic said. "That's brilliant. That's what we call asymmetrical warfare."

"Really?" I asked. I was intrigued.

"Definitely," he said. "The genius of the playground is that it can't be co-opted by local militia. There are stories of organizations building new schools in Afghanistan, and then a few months later the schools are taken over and used by the Taliban as bases for their ongoing operation. What happens next? The US military bombs the school to get rid of the Taliban, and you're back to square one. You have to be careful about the kinds of things you're bringing into play in these environments."

"I never thought of that," I said.

"The other thing I like about the playground idea is that children are not afforded a place to play in these war zones. There's no safe place. The schools have been destroyed. This means mothers never get a break. If you build a playground, it becomes a de facto child care facility. The moms can all come to one central place, and one mom might ask another mom, 'Can you watch my kids while I go take a break?' Now the kids are playing together."

"That's so true," I said. I hadn't even thought through these elements of the playgrounds. The idea simply resonated with me. But Nic kept going.

"The whole concept of play in the Middle East usually comes down to one of two things: Either kids are playing a sport like soccer, or they're playing war."

"We definitely saw that," I said, telling him the story of Aram.

"There's just not much in between sports and war," he explained. "So few children have access to a playground. But I can see how they might start to build bridges, you know? The locals start to see the US and US organizations as being a positive force within Islamic culture.

Of course, these are just the positive second-order effects, but there are also negative ones that you have to be aware of. The bottom line is, if you can make a positive impact on the women in the Islamic culture, you will impact the entire culture."

"How do you know this stuff?"

"I used to work for the CIA," Nic said. "Now I'm in the nonprofit world."

"Really," I said.

He nodded.

"Listen, I think you're on to something," he said. "If you want me to, I can put you in contact with people who can scout out the area, negotiate the playground with key people, make sure the playground goes up as planned. There's a lot of money that disappears in these areas if you're not careful."

"I'd love to talk more," I said.

"Here's the thing. Some NGOs just want to make a video, but they don't care about the long-term effects. I can't be involved if you are just providing something that has tangible value. You need to be providing things that are subjectively valuable as well, something the community values as a whole but doesn't make anyone wealthier. That's why I love this playground idea so much."

I was intrigued. If this guy with experience in the Middle East thought playgrounds were a good idea, then I thought, *Let's do it!*

But at this point building multiple playgrounds in war-torn areas was still only a vision.

During the next few weeks I considered Nic's offer, and we met again. The more we spoke, the more sold I was on his way of doing things. Within a few weeks of us meeting, he was meeting with Skip, and I was thinking, *Skip is busy and it's hard to get onto his calendar for a one-on-one meeting.* The next week I met Nic's fiancé, and she was dressed in clothes from my favorite store.

Has he been doing research on me? I wondered. *Are they trying to ingratiate themselves with me? She likes everything I like! I love working out and had been training at a gym for the trip to Burma. She was a personal trainer and life coach. It seemed too good to be true.*

One night Skip and I were in bed, and I was telling him about all these things going on with Nic, how he was so helpful but also how his background brought out my inner conspiracy theorist.

"He might still be with the CIA," I said. "You just wait. Soon we're going to have a crisis in our lives only Nic can fix."

"Lenya," Skip said without looking up from his book, "you've been watching too many movies."

"I can't do covert," I said to Skip, turning out my light. "I am going to have to be direct."

I invited Nic to lunch. We sat down together at the table, and I didn't beat around the bush. "Nic, I find myself in a situation where I have no way of verifying that you are who you say you are."

He nodded. "That's true, Lenya. You will only find a few references to me on the Internet." He gave me a short list of places his name would come up if I did a search, and he was right. I had already done that search.

"This is a problem for me, Nic. I'm starting to introduce you to people, but I have no way of verifying who you are."

"I can see why this would be an issue," he said, smiling.

"So, this is where I am," I said, and I was serious. "I can't verify you. All I can say is, I know God. And I know God's voice. He talks to me, and sometimes I ask Him questions. I ask Him a lot about you. If God ever tells me there is a red flag with Nic McKinley, I will drop you like a hot potato."

Yes, I said this to an ex-CIA agent. But he wasn't bothered at all.

"First of all," Nic said with a half smile on his face, "I love God too. I pray that if God ever tells you something about me, you will tell me first. But I get your concerns. I have a dossier with enough info for you to properly vet me. You can see who I am and what training I've had. I can let you see a copy of that. I can even let you keep a copy, but I'd ask that you not keep it in your office. It needs to stay in your house."

"Why the house?" I asked.

"Quite frankly, I've been in your office. I could break in there in two minutes and you'd never know I was even there."

"Nick," I said in a serious voice, "how many times have you been in my office?"

We both laughed.

Nic asked me, "What do you want to do next? What's your long-term plan?"

"Honestly," I admitted, "I know this sounds naïve, but I follow the Holy Spirit. When I look at my life now, there's no way I could have envisioned doing this five years ago. Yet here I am. How could I have planned for this?"

"I understand that," he said. "But you need to think about the placement of your playgrounds. It's going to be important that you place them strategically."

He pulled out a napkin and spread it on the table in between us. Then he took a straw and dropped one drop of water on the napkin.

"That's your playground," he said.

And he placed another drop close to that one. And another close to those. And another.

"See how the circles spread? They overlap quickly, and they cover a certain area. But what if you do this?"

He got a new napkin. This time he spread the drops out really far apart, but as they spread they came close to touching, and this time they covered a much larger area.

"See what I'm saying? If you're too close together, you lose out on potential influence."

As I was meeting with Nic and trying to determine how to move forward, we were also looking at where we were going to get our playground materials.

Originally we were going to purchase old army junk and build the playgrounds from scratch. But Murray, who was basically our head of construction, kept asking, "Can't we just buy a normal child's playground from Turkey and ship it in?"

"No, Murray, I like the idea of repurposing old military equipment," I repeatedly answered.

Murray kept pushing his idea of sourcing the playgrounds locally. Eventually I thought he was going to drive me crazy.

"Seriously, Murray! I will thump you if you keep on about this. We're building them ourselves. Don't bring it up again!"

That is, until one day we found out there was a guy in Erbil, Kurdistan, who sold playgrounds. And another friend put us in contact with a place here in the States where we could buy used playgrounds at a steep discount. So we kept looking around, but we were definitely moving in the direction of what Murray had wanted all along: using playground suppliers.

We decided to build our first one in the Tohlakai community on the Navajo Nation reservation in New Mexico as a way of helping the children there. It would also be a practice run to see if Murray could take one of these playgrounds out of its box and put it together. Murray went out to the reservation on a cold, blustery day. The semi couldn't even make it all the way down the dirt roads. They had no ladders or scaffolding, so he had to stand on the crates to build the higher sections of the playground. But all credit to Murray—he got it done with the help of the locals and volunteers from our church in Albuquerque.

The playground went up around Christmastime, and it was beautiful. We took a trip out there after it was constructed. The reservation was so rundown, and the people were living in such abject poverty. It was sad. But before I knew it, kids were coming out of the wilderness from every direction to play on the playground. Thirty or so showed up for the grand opening, and we sang and dedicated it. Then the pastor of the local church, Calvary Tohlakai, showed up, and he loved it.

Then a hundred more children showed up. I realized in that moment that if we could partner with the right people, a playground could be the very tool they needed to reach their community. Standing there on that windswept reservation, hearing the children laughing, watching them play, I saw something else: Nic had been right.

There were moms everywhere.

What an incredible confirmation that first playground was for us. This might work! As the weeks passed, we found out that even children from outside the reservation were going to the playground to play.

To top it off, we met a jeweler there named Landoll who made a new piece of jewelry for the Reload Love collection. It was a beautiful piece in the shape of a feather. Could God in His economy use these playgrounds to help people at every level? Could Reload Love not only supply playgrounds but also help someone like Landoll make a better life for himself and his community?

Every tribe and nation.

The Karen people of Burma.

The Yazidi people of Iraq.

And right there in our backyard, in New Mexico, the Tohlakai.

Once again God was illustrating to me His faithfulness to every tribe, every nation, and I was in awe.

It was time for Reload Love to go to the Middle East.

PART FOUR

Forgiveness in the Rubble

Forgive us our debts, as we forgive our debtors.

MATTHEW 6:12

9

The Gift of a Small Wooden Cross

April 2017

We drive through the rubble ISIS left behind when they retreated months earlier, deep into an Assyrian Christian city of Iraq called Qaraqosh, population 50,000. At least, before ISIS that was the population. Now the city is vacant. It is hard to believe this is the same day we walked through ISIS tunnels, the same day we went down into the darkness and walked the same paths as those who have caused such terror. But it is. The same empty breeze blowing. The same checkpoints and endless fields of something green. Hay? Barley?

By now it was in the afternoon, though the low, gray sky made it hard to tell what time it was. Our Shocker pulls to a stop in front of a building that is barely recognizable as a church—there are large, imposing doors, still in place, and a bell tower that stands out in stark relief above the rest of the destruction. The spaces in the bell tower are jagged from where chunks have been shot out, and the bell seems to be hanging on by a thread. The whole structure around the bell looks like it might collapse at any moment. There are ornate carvings in the stone, decorated pillars, and archways.

There are soldiers everywhere, old men and young, each with large automatic weapons slung over their shoulders. Their eyes are dark and tired and hard to read. They stare at us as we drive up, a van full of Americans. I wonder if they resent our smiles, our Westernness, our presence? It is so hard to tell. Many of the soldiers previously seemed to welcome us. Some asked us to tell our fellow Americans they needed more help fighting ISIS. It seems impossible to guess what someone might think of us—the responses are so varied.

It is curious to me that just as we come to a stop and start getting out of the van, an entirely different entourage pulls in beside us, coming from the opposite direction. I hear someone say that the Assyrian church dignitaries are returning to the Qaraqosh area. I saw a video showing their return during Holy Week for Palm Sunday and Easter, and it makes me feel a little more relaxed, knowing that these people think it's safe to be here.

But I also feel reverential and emotional, seeing someone dressed like a bishop or a priest climb up out of a black Mercedes with tinted windows. He stares up at the belfry. He looks around at the devastation, his face an empty slate. The entire neighborhood is rubble. It is difficult to explain unless you have been in a war zone. It feels like the end of the world has come and gone, and we are among those who remain.

We walk toward the church, and this bishop, this important man, shakes hands with each of us, nodding his head, saying something in his own language. I nod and smile back. Now that I'm out of the van, I can see even more soldiers. It's amazing to me how many militia are in the area. So many different uniforms, so many different colors, and they all stand separated by type, each with his own. I don't know the players here. Who is a good guy? Are there any bad guys? Are there any here who would take us away and sell us for ransom money? Will fighting break out between them? There seems to be a rank and file, but not knowing what rank and file each soldier is, well, that feels like a disadvantage.

The doors are open, but the inside of the church is unlit and looks unnaturally dark. Our group walks toward the steps, and we follow the dignitary inside. The steps are so crowded with soldiers that they have to turn to the side to let us pass. Some of them are smoking. Some are looking around. It is eerily silent, and our footsteps over the rock and dust are loud.

Walking inside the church, one phrase comes to my mind.

The abomination of desolation.

It seems something sacred has been irreparably marred. Those ancient places of worship have a particular grandeur we don't often see in the United States. Perhaps we get a sense of it with the Statue of Liberty or the great memorials we have put in place in Washington, DC, or the older churches you find in Boston or New York. Imagine if the Statue of Liberty's face was removed, or if Abraham Lincoln's stone statue was somehow disfigured, his head taken off.

This is what ISIS did to the church building.

Inside, the church is black. The walls have been scorched. Someone explains to us that in order to burn the stone inside the church, ISIS created a kind of pitch, some kind of flammable composition, and spread it around. You have to be highly motivated to spend time burning something that is not flammable, something like marble or granite. The walls are black from the fire that someone tells us burned for days. When the church was burning, the rising smoke was a constant reminder of what was lost. Now the blackness inside is something they are fighting to overcome.

Immediately inside the door are these huge columns, so large it would take three or four of us with our arms outstretched to reach around them. They are black as well, with chunks ripped out and craters from bullets. But they're still impressive. The architecture of those old churches was meant to give the congregant a specific kind of experience, a desire to look up, and those columns feel so stable, so permanent, even in the middle of this war zone. They stood strong. The columns remained.

I think of the two columns in the temple in Jerusalem, the bronze ones that Solomon built and named. I think of the old saying, "If walls could talk," but in this case I wonder, *What if pillars could talk? What strange and beautiful things have these two columns seen through the years? What atrocities? What sadness?* I try to imagine all the people who have entered the church under their towering presence.

They, too, stood through war and unimaginable horrors. They, too, bore witness.

I am overwhelmed by how many seasons in history there have been when people have tried to extinguish the church. I think of Russia and China and more ancient cultures. I think of all the ways Jerusalem has withstood being destroyed.

Yet God remains faithful, and there is always a remnant.

I think of Noah in his boat, Lot fleeing Sodom, and the Israelites going to Babylon. It is a common thread of Christian history. There is always a remnant. Even here in Iraq, even in the rubble and destruction ISIS left in their wake, a remnant of Christians remains.

Murray puts his hands up on one of the pillars, and I can see him whispering.

"Jesus, Jesus, Jesus."

Outside, before we came into the church, in the city that surrounds us, I did not see anyone other than soldiers. I did not see any inhabitable houses or families walking the streets. All of the businesses were blown to pieces, their metal shutters bent in or pried off. Yet here, in this church in Qaraqosh, the bishop leads a service, and Christians have gathered. I can hear him speaking, and the congregation responding, and I can only think of one thing.

Blessed is he who comes in the name of the Lord.

We walk quietly to about halfway up the church sanctuary and then turn right to walk into the courtyard. The church is so large that no one participating in the service turns to look at us. I read about this church's courtyard before I came, but I was not expecting something quite so grand. We walk in between more pillars, down a few steps, and enter this wide-open space flanked by two buildings. At the far end, there are multiple arches that lead out to another rubble-strewn street.

In the middle of the courtyard is a pile of ashes. Someone tells me that is where they burned the Bibles. You cannot understand what a desecration that is unless you understand how a Muslim person handles the Koran. A Muslim person will never let the Koran touch the ground. They treat it with a physical respect, place it on the highest shelf, sometimes wrapping it in cloth to protect it. Even the ISIS flag is treated with a great deal of respect by many because it has the word *Allah* on it. We, on the other hand, take our Bibles for granted. Most Christians in America probably have at least five of them and think very little about the holiness of those physical pages.

But this destruction, it wasn't just a temporary attempt to push back Christianity—their goal is to eliminate an entire culture, an entire religion. Everything that was done in this church was done with purpose and with a message in mind. This has gone on for centuries, not just in the Middle East, but all around the world. ISIS's goal was nothing less than complete annihilation of Christianity.

Yet there is always a remnant.

At the other end of the courtyard, there is a kind of pulpit that has been shot to bits, and there are mannequins standing, also shot to pieces. This place of peace was used as a firing range. There are reports that Christians were beheaded or crucified here.

The abomination of desolation.

It was only three years earlier that ISIS flooded through Sinjar and moved through Mosul. We watched on the news as city after city fell— Qaraqosh fell in a day. We watched, wondering why no one was doing anything, why they were allowed to advance so quickly.

I squat down and stare at the floor of the courtyard. I reach down and pick up a bullet casing. I suddenly realize there are tons of them all around me, scattered under my feet like pebbles. I gather a handful and put them in my pocket. Bullets to beauty. Reload love. I feel like we are so close to the heart of our mission.

I look up at the roof of the church and can see the belfry again. I remember the story I had heard from Dr. Bashar, how a mortar hit his street and two children in the neighborhood were killed. He and his family had made a horrific journey across the desert. I couldn't believe we were walking the streets of his hometown. He had told me one of the most chilling things I have ever heard.

"I have no past," he said, and he meant that he had other family members, a business, a home. He had his own private clinic and did work for the government at the hospital, but when ISIS showed up and gave everyone three hours to leave, he lost everything.

He said that the bell had historically been rung when bad things were happening as a warning to the community. When the rumors came that ISIS was coming, he sent his wife and remaining children into the desert to wait for him. When he saw the nuns grabbing children and running, he knew it was no joke, it was no false alarm. They left, and his past was obliterated.

They wondered if the church would stand.

But here it is.

I'm thinking of this city, thinking of the people who fled, when we turn into one of the long buildings that forms one of the sides of the courtyard. It is one of the stone residences, where Sister Diana, a dear servant of God, had her room. This was also the building where the orphans stayed, where they were taught and fed and taken care of. Walking in, this building seems more destroyed than anything else I have seen. There is a picture of Jesus on the floor with shattered glass around it.

We go around the corner and enter a small room. Ceiling tiles dangle down above us, clinging to their wires. Everything is covered in a thin film of white dust. A priest is digging through the rubble of broken ceiling tiles and pieces of stone and piles of supplies that had been flung out of the closet in the search for something valuable. Plastic is melted. The ceiling fan is melted. The debris is knee-high in some areas of the room.

I feel like an interloper, watching the priest and two nuns going through the rubble piece by piece. I feel out of place. I came around the corner, and this is what I have walked into: some kind of retrieval effort. Some kind of new tragedy.

Oh my. We either need to leave or we need to help. Back out slowly, or figure out what they are doing.

I turn toward Shocker.

"What are they doing?" I ask in a firm voice. We did not come all this way to stand idly by. "What can we do to help?"

That's when I notice the priest is holding a kind of purple board to his chest while using the other hand to look through the rubble. He pulls out flannel graph characters from the mess: David, Moses, Jesus, a group of little children. A cross. A large stone.

There is always a remnant.

Shocker asks him what they are doing, and he answers.

"We are missing half of our flannel board," he says in a quiet voice, without emotion. His eyes are like pools of still water. "This is how we teach the children about Jesus, and this is our only one. They don't sell these in our country. We must find the other half."

He bends over and continues his search. We help him for a little while, looking around the edges, picking up large boards and moving things from here to there.

"We'll find one for you in the US and mail it here," I say. "We can help with that."

Shocker tells the man in his own language what I have said, that we will make sure he has a flannel board. A flannel board! Such a small thing to us, such a monumental thing to this father of orphans. Shocker goes on to tell the priest that we understand, that we grieve with him. Shocker is trying to tell him that we sympathize with what they've gone through, but the priest looks up and says something in a firm voice. He is not angry, but he talks with confidence.

I ask Shocker what the priest said.

"He said, 'No, I don't think you do know how I feel.'"

But he pauses before continuing.

"The priest also said, 'We will not let hate win here. We will forgive these people,'" and he gestures at the chaos, the destruction. "He said, 'We will forgive them. We pray only that God can change their hearts and that we can bring the children back here to teach them about love and forgiveness because that is the only future.'"

I stand there holding rubble in my hand, and I want to sob. The entire time I walked around the church, all I could think about was how terrible these people were who had done this—damaged the church! Killed Christians! Forced out the orphans! That day we had seen the X-ray of a bullet millimeters from a young girl's heart; we saw a child crying for her mother who had been killed; we saw injured children trying to clap their bandaged hands. We sang with the children in the hospital.

Yet here this priest stands, wanting to forgive, more willing than I was to move on, to seek peace.

"We will teach the children about love and forgiveness, because that is the only future."

This is a day that will take a long time for me to process. This is a day that needs to settle deep into my soul.

I see a box of tiny wooden crosses on the floor, some scattered around in the debris. I pick up five of them for our Reload Love team, then ask the priest if I can have them. He nods. He smiles. I put them in my pocket.

When we walk out, a soldier stops us. At first I am a little bit nervous, but he only asks if we will take a picture with him, so we do, there on the steps outside the sanctuary, at the edge of the courtyard. We try to smile, but the smiles come weak and watered-down. Behind us, the firing range, the pile of ashes, the arches with their bullet-hole divots.

Snap goes the camera.

Snap.

Snap.

The soldier smiles a bashful grin, and I suddenly realize how young he is. Sixteen? Eighteen? Twenty-one? The gun strap shifts awkwardly on his shoulder, his AK47 swinging like a toy gun. I blink my eyes and shake my head. Surely this is a dream. Surely this is a nightmare.

We drive away through the rubble-filled streets, and in the van we are all quiet. It lurches in and out of potholes. The reflection of destroyed buildings flashes past in the window, and in that moment, as we drive away, I see the first family I have seen in Qaraqosh.

They are walking toward the church: a mother, a father, and two children. One of the children rides on his father's shoulders, the father holding tightly to his small feet. I wonder if the streets are safe. Again, I think back to the training we had received only the day before, the training about the landmines and the IEDs left lying around for children to find, to detonate. Could it be possible that training was only 24 hours ago?

I turn my head and watch the family as they grow smaller behind us and turn to go into the church. The Christians are returning. A remnant is still here. The Lord will be faithful to even this generation.

I know I want to come back to this place. I want to build a playground that will serve the children, one that will bring even more little ones to hear the priest's unforgettable message of forgiveness. If there is a man in this city still teaching about forgiveness, even after all that has happened, I want to support that man.

10

Mafraq Is Not to Be Trifled With

The word *sensual* doesn't mean sexual, though that's how many of us hear it. *Sensual* means fleshly. The deep flesh. When that word came to mind recently, I jumped to James and read about the contrast of wisdom from above versus wisdom from below. The latter is self-seeking and divisive. It is earthly, demonic.

In December of 2015, I made my first trip to the Middle East, this time to Jordan to meet with someone in the city of Mafraq. Reload Love was growing in leaps and bounds, and we had seriously begun the work of building playgrounds in communities impacted by terror. We had decided that would be our focus, our direction.

But I came into this new mission in Mafraq woefully unprepared, especially in one area. I failed to take to heart my own teaching on Ephesians and specifically that our struggle is not with flesh and blood but with principalities and powers. We were prepared to pray against the black banners of ISIS, but I did not recognize or prepare for the fact that we would be going up against a spirit of division within our own team.

I quickly learned that the unseen forces in Mafraq were not to be trifled with.

To get to Mafraq, you must leave Amman and drive north, toward Syria, and through the Jordanian wilderness. It is barren and dusty, the dirt a light tan color, completely dry. The only things in sight are bare shrubs that look like tumbleweed, outcroppings of rocks, and the thin horizon where the pale-blue sky meets the almost-white dust. Drive through this for a few hours, and up out of nowhere, Mafraq appears. There, the buildings, the sidewalks, and the streets are the same color as the dust.

This was a new venture for me. In this situation I was no longer the pastor's wife. I was at the top, leading the charge, and in a place as patriarchal as the Middle East, this can mess with you. I had to make a serious adjustment. I was also wearing multiple hats on that first trip: We were trying to get a film in the can we could use to promote Reload Love; we had fund-raised for a bus and sponsored 30 children to go to school, so I was an ambassador to the school's administration; and we were scoping out potential playground locations.

Arriving in Mafraq, I could feel an undercurrent of tension. First of all, there was tension in the streets. People stared at our van full of Westerners, their faces empty of emotion. I could only guess what they thought about us. Our van pulled through a large iron gate and onto the church property, the gate clanging behind us.

But there was also tension within the team, and especially with one particular team member. I kept asking Jen if she thought everything was okay.

"I feel this tension I can't explain," I said.

"No," Jen assured me. "It's okay. There are some things going on, but it will be fine."

We walked into the church building, and I got to meet Pastor Nour. He is gentle and kind and welcomed us with that typical Middle Eastern hospitality. He had been in that city for a long time, and he had the respect and trust of the local authorities. We wanted to do some filming, and I planned on talking with him about how we could further help the children, mostly refugees, at a nearby school. We also wanted to support his mission by building some playgrounds.

There was a gentleman brought in to add stronger security measures, but it added another layer of tension to everything because he was constantly asking questions and making suggestions about what was safe and what was not. We did some filming. Talked to the kids. Talked to the pastor. Then we walked into a room filled with Syrian refugee women. It was made clear that we needed to be extra gentle with them—they were new to the country and had been through hell.

We walked in tentative, careful. The film crew caught some of it, but they needed to move on.

"Please stay with us!" the women said to me. "Please stay and eat with us!"

I decided to let the film crew continue getting B-roll and doing interviews while Jen, another woman, and I stayed and ate with these refugee women. I made that audible without thinking. Everything felt chaotic and disjointed that day. I didn't think about how I was separating a fourth woman from us. I thought I was being deferential by keeping her on the film team. But that decision had ramifications.

We sat with the women and listened to their stories. As soon as the film crew left, they took off their veils, came out from behind them as if they were shedding masks. They wanted to come over and sit close, hold our arms in their hands and touch our faces. They wanted us to take photos with them. They opened up and told us their stories.

One of the women shared a story about her sons. The two boys had been walking down a street in their Syrian village, holding hands, when a sniper shot and killed one of the boys. The boy who survived stood there and stared at his dead brother. He didn't know what to do.

"My son has not spoken since the shooting," she said, tears in her eyes.

Another woman told us of her uncle, how he was taken and tortured and then returned to them, unable to speak or move or live on his own. Every single one of them had a story about a relative or a friend who had been killed or maimed or tortured. And what, to them, was worst of all? The division that took place in their communities.

"In the end, when we decided to leave, you could not trust your neighbor," one of the women said. "It was everyone looking out for themselves. You did not know who was a government informer, who was a rebel. You did not know who the enemy was. Anyone could turn you in, even an old friend."

Division was a spirit that had roamed the streets of their Syrian towns, and now it prowled the streets of Mafraq.

We could have easily spent the rest of the day with them. Their stories were heartbreaking. They offered their friendship to us unconditionally. But we had to move on.

As we left, Jen turned to me.

"I think we might have a problem." She explained that the woman I had left out, the one who had gone with the film crew, was upset I hadn't asked her to stay with us. I sensed something was off but didn't realize it would reach critical mass so quickly. The rest of the team went downstairs while I said a final good-bye to the women. We were still supposed to go sit with Pastor Nour, whom I had just met, as well as spend some time with another person, and finally, visit the school. But by the time I got downstairs, the plans had changed.

"You're in big trouble," another team member told me as I came down. "The producer is frustrated and the woman is fuming. Everyone is in the van, ready to leave. Apparently we're going back to Amman now."

"What?" I asked, completely taken aback.

"He said he has everything he needs. We're leaving."

I didn't know what to say. I was so surprised by this dissent that I capitulated, although in hindsight I don't think I should have. Pastor Nour came around the corner, expecting us to stay and chat more with him. He was looking forward to telling us about his mission and the school, and I wanted to talk to him about playgrounds.

"No, I'm sorry," I said, still shell-shocked. "We have to leave."

"What about the school?" he asked.

"No, I'm sorry," I said again, not knowing how to explain what was happening.

I got in the van, and we left.

I won't go into any more details. There were many difficult conversations over the next few months, and I had to explore what it meant for me to lead this growing thing called Reload Love. The division didn't stay in Mafraq either—it followed me back to Albuquerque and, for a while, it persisted.

We went there unprepared for what we would face spiritually, and the repercussions were long-lasting. Our team was confronted with the sensual, the factious, the divisive—that is to say, the flesh, the demonic—and because we weren't prepared, it caused devastation to that trip that might not have been undone without the grace and mercy of Pastor Nour and my Reload Love teammates.

We encountered it again on subsequent trips too: Our first team to go over and build playgrounds was almost arrested on the street for taking photographs. The second team arrived as a volunteer at the church had a nervous breakdown. Later a member of our team mishandled pain medication and was sidelined.

This is a precautionary tale for any organization. There are spiritual landmines, and you need to be rooted in prayer if you want to discern their whereabouts. We do not wrestle with flesh and blood but principalities and powers. We have to know the enemy is pushing, prodding, poking. We have to be prepared for what we might face.

During our most recent trip to Mafraq, I had the opportunity to sit down and speak with Pastor Nour again. He is such a kind man, and he bears deep spiritual wisdom. I want to share his words here with you.

I am not originally from Mafraq—I was born in Jericho in the west bank of the Jordan River in 1965. My father was a policeman working for the Jordanian government. In 1967, when I was still a baby, there was the war with Israel, and we fled to Jordan. Once we arrived, they appointed my father as a policeman in Mafraq. I do not believe this happened by accident. I am in Mafraq for a purpose.

Now I am like a fish. The fish can't go from water, and I can't go from Mafraq. When God calls us to a place, stay there until called somewhere else. He doesn't need me to remind Him, to ask what's next. I stay in my place until He says where and when I should go. Stay. Stay here. When He wants me to go to another place, He will tell me.

My vision of reaching people is still the same, but the way to do it is always changing. The main goal is to reach out to the people around us. How do we do that? Using different tools. The main goal is to be able to connect with the people around us and share with them the Word of God.

There are 70,000 Jordanians in Mafraq and 100,000 Syrian refugees. The Jordanians are kind and peaceful people with tribal backgrounds. They give value to the tribe. They are not fanatical Muslims. We have good relationships with them as the church. We are respected because they know we help the people. We don't take advantage of anyone.

For most people, it is hard to stay here. There is nothing here for the new generation unless they are called by God to stay. Some go to America, others go to other places. They want a dream. Usually they find nothing. There were 15 to 20 young men in this church in the early days, and I am the only one left.

I remember when Reload Love first came here and spent time with the women, asking questions, listening. I was happy because the women opened up and told their stories. They were traumatized. I could feel their emotion. Lenya was timid to ask them questions because we could feel it was heavy, but I always tell my people not only to listen but to tell their own stories. This way they know it's not just them and their pain. Everyone has their own struggles. Hearing the stories of others brings hope to the hearer.

What would I say to Christians in the United States? Welcoming refugees is a great chance for you to reach the people around you. Don't be afraid of them. If you remain afraid, then they become a threat, but if you go to them with the love of the Lord, you will no longer be afraid. Jesus died for them. Love them. Don't wait for them to come to your churches—go to their houses. Show them love and respect. When an American visits a Syrian family, this means you are saying they are welcome. You love them.

I know you have beautiful churches with gymnasiums and community centers. Open it to them. If it becomes dirty, clean it. Don't be afraid. Let them come and destroy it with use, and then replace it. Use it. Don't worship it. So much money is used to entertain the Christians in the churches, and too many pastors have become entertainers. All of these resources should be used to help people and share the gospel.

Open your eyes. Is there space for people in your life, or are you just doing things? Family things? Church things? Is there a place for people to come to us from time to time, different people? Do you have time for them? Is there a place for them too?

Dedicate your lives to them. Pray, and your service will define your life. God will make your life busy, but with people who need you.

Pastor Nour is a man who says yes. When a group of Canadians came to him and offered computers, even though few people knew how to use them, he said yes. Now they give computer classes at the church. When Europeans wanted to supply a sewing room, he said yes, and now they teach refugee women how to sew. When Americans wanted to provide tables and chairs, he said yes.

This always results in added work for Pastor Nour, but when God presents him with an opportunity, even one he doesn't understand, he says yes. He has said yes to volunteers coming to his church and yes to refugees and yes to helping the locals. He has said yes so many times that he has had to hire someone to administer all of these yeses.

But do you know what else Pastor Nour taught me about saying yes? He taught me that when someone who might appear to have less than we do offers us something, it is important to accept their offering. It is important to say yes when someone wants to be hospitable, to give you their food or their seat or their space. Pastor Nour taught us that to say yes when a refugee offers you their food, even if it is the last thing they have in the house, is one way of restoring dignity to people who have been stripped of almost everything else.

There were many times during my trips to the Middle East when someone gave me something I knew they could not afford to give me. My instinct was to say, "No! Please! This means more to you than it does to me. Keep it." But Pastor Nour showed us at his church in Mafraq that receiving is a kind of giving, that accepting hospitality is actually a way of being hospitable. I will not forget this.

Say yes to those who offer hospitality to you. Say yes to God when a door opens. Then keep moving forward.

11

To Sinjar...Almost

It was now June 2016, just 15 months since Skip had taken our Love Bomb money to Iraq, and I was finally going over to meet the people and organizations we were partnering with. Murray and videographer Nick had gone over ahead of us to Jordan to build playgrounds for Pastor Nour in Mafraq and they would meet us in Iraq. By this time we were completely into the playground-building phase, and we had partnered with an organization called Kids Around the World to help supply the playground equipment.

I couldn't wait to get to Iraq. I was flying from a meeting in Hawaii, to Los Angeles, to Chicago where I planned on meeting the team. Then we'd fly together to Istanbul and finally to Erbil. But one of the flights was delayed, which meant I didn't get to Chicago in time to head over with the team. I was so bummed. I would have to fly to the Middle East on my own.

I was also a little apprehensive about traveling without Jen. We go everywhere together, and it's a safety measure God has given to me. Jen and I are both on such similar wavelengths, and if anything comes up that is out of the ordinary or that we have to make a snap decision about, one way I can discern God's will is by seeing how God is speaking to Jen. We go into things united, and if there's disagreement, we know to stop and explore what's going on.

I had made a mad dash to Chicago International, but by the time I arrived, the flight was long gone, so I went back to the desk to find another flight. The woman working behind the desk was nice.

"Okay," she said, "because it's our fault you didn't make your connection, we'll put you up in a hotel."

I was so tired by this point. Exhausted. I wasn't happy about having to stay in Chicago by myself. And I so badly wanted to be with the team.

"If I was your daughter, which hotel would you put me in?" I asked her, smiling. I really didn't want to end up in some dump, and I think we all think differently, myself included, when we see people as our family.

She started crying.

"My daughter is dead," she said quietly. "I would do anything to put my daughter up in a hotel."

She made my arrangements, put me in a cab, and I ended up at this super nice place. She had called her manager, and they put me up in the hotel where the pilots and flight attendants stay. Not only that, but she put me in a suite and got me breakfast on their dime. She was such a kind woman, and I thought of her the whole time I stayed there.

The next day I boarded a flight from Chicago to Istanbul, and then from Istanbul to Erbil, Kurdistan, in northern Iraq. That was a long day of flying, and I was feeling travel worn by the time the plane got close to Erbil, so I went into the bathroom to try and freshen up. I got out my hairspray and did my hair, and wouldn't you know it, the hairspray set off the alarm in the airplane's bathroom. I heard feet running down the aisle toward me, and then someone was banging on the bathroom door.

Bam, bam, bam!

Oh no, they think I'm a terrorist.

I opened the door.

"Hairspray!" I said nervously. "It's just my hairspray!"

They were furious.

"I'm sorry!" I said over and over again. "I'm so sorry! I had no idea."

These are the kinds of things that happen to me when I travel. This was my welcome to Iraq.

Once I met up with the team, who were waiting for me at the airport, we headed for the IDP camp run by Father Douglas, one of the IDP camps Skip had visited 15 months before. Father Douglas greeted us when we arrived, but he seemed tired. Discouraged.

He had been through so much during his years as a priest. Before escaping and coming to run the IDP camp, he had spent nine days tied up by ISIS. During the day, he served as a spiritual father to his captors! One of them was always asking Father Douglas about his wife, always looking for relationship advice.

"Tell her 'Good morning' from time to time," Father Douglas encouraged him. "Leave her kind messages."

But not all of his captors saw him as a holy man. They took him into a very clean room and turned up the volume of a Muslim station, demanding he renounce his faith in Christ. Then, when he would not, they got out a hammer and hit him in the face. One of his teeth flew out. The guard picked it up.

"Do not worry," the man said, leering at him. "You have many teeth. We have all night."

Father Douglas told us this story in a resigned voice.

"As priests," he said, "we know we will not die a normal death. We will not die of old age. So we give our wills to other priests."

He pointed at a wall in his office, and it was covered with the banners of other NGOs.

"Do you want to know who has helped us?" he asked in a solemn voice. "These are the people who have helped."

He gave us a tour of the camp, and he was a lovely man, but he was withdrawn and quiet. I could tell he had done a lot of good with the money we had given him, but he seemed to be discouraged about the direction his country was taking. I could not blame him. Years and years of violence and "an eye for an eye" can erode even the strongest of hopes.

Then there was the time on this trip when I was able to share the gospel with Baba Chawish, the venerated religious leader of the Yazidi people.

We drove into Lalish, the 4,000-year-old religious center of the Yazidi people, a village tucked away in the valleys and mountains of northern Iraq. We were ushered into a long, creamy white room and given seats. Baba Chawish is like the pope for the Yazidis, and his influence within the community is unmatched. These are the same Yazidis I had seen on television, starving on Mount Sinjar. If we wanted to help them, having his blessing would be invaluable.

We sat there, waiting, and he walked into the room with his entourage. He is one of the most imposing men I've ever met: tall, with dark, piercing eyes and a huge beard. He seemed massive in his white turban and white robe. He had an aura about him, and when he spoke, his deep voice was interpreted for us by one of his assistants.

He began by explaining the background of his people, the Yazidis. They believe in a gradual process of purification through reincarnation. You cannot convert to be a Yazidi—only those born into the group are accepted in their culture. They do not wear the color blue because it is a holy color. They venerate the sun and consider fire sacred. They celebrate the new year in April with colored eggs. Listening to him, and having read up a little bit about their religion, it seemed to me their beliefs are an amalgamation of Judaism, Christianity, and Zoroastrianism. Historically they were very secretive and only recently opened their doors to outsiders.

We listened politely, and when he had finished, I spoke up.

"Baba Chawish, we believe in the son too, but we believe in the Son of God. Our Scriptures say He is the light of the world, one who shines brighter than the sun itself. In the last days, when the sun and the moon disappear, it will be His light that sheds light on the world. This Son of God has told us that as His children, we should reflect His light, that our good deeds make light, and that if we want to reflect Him, we must do good deeds for others."

I paused. His dark, imposing eyes seemed open to what I was saying. He and his assistants sat there listening. It was a beautiful moment, this conversation we were having, this open exchange of world views.

"So we are here to show you this light, the light of God's Son, Jesus. To show you this light, we would love to build you a playground."

He nodded thoughtfully. "We will need more than one playground."

When we had finished speaking, the man who was his primary spokesman or chief of staff gave us a tour of their temple, and it was one of the more fascinating places I've ever been inside. Outside the door to the temple was the image of a black, twisting snake, and in order to enter, we had to duck down. This sort of enforced humbling seems typical of many pagan temples.

But just as we were about to bend forward and go inside, a white snake came sliding out through the door. Everyone around us got excited and started exclaiming to each other, "White snake! Look at the white snake!" The Yazidis are a superstitious people, and the sight of this white snake, in direct opposition to the black snake above the door, had them excited. It was in no hurry, this pale serpent, and it reminded me of when Moses' staff turned into a snake and ate the staffs of the Egyptian magicians.

"I've never seen a white snake before," someone whispered.

It slowly slithered up and away from the door, and we crouched and went inside. We came into a dark, sooty, smelly area, kind of an open room with stone walls and columns. A rag hung down from the ceiling, an old piece of fabric tied in a knot.

"If you untie the knot," our guide explained, "you release the prayer of the person who came before you. Then you can say a prayer and tie the knot. Your prayer will be released by the next person who comes and unties it."

"This is rather complicated and superstitious," I whispered to Jen, and we continued deeper into the temple. Someone in our group started to question us being there—the whole place felt dark and foreboding.

At that very moment, I heard the most horrific screaming I have ever heard in my life, followed by the wailing of women. The wailing reminded me of the mourning I read about in the Bible, the kind of mourning I'd never heard before in person. I walked straight toward the sound, needing to see what was going on. The other female teammates, Jen and Jolene, a quiet, powerful woman whose husband served in the Albuquerque police department, followed close behind.

A woman came around the corner, slapping herself on the body and face. She screamed the most awful screams. I was shocked. Women followed behind her, crying and wailing and screaming. The sounds they made were otherworldly, almost supernatural. Our interpreter walked over and asked one of the women what was going on.

The screaming woman had just found out that ISIS had killed her son. This was her grief.

Do not look away, I sensed a voice saying to me. *See what is going on.*

We watched as they made their way through the room, leaving us behind.

The next day we drove to Khanke Camp to visit the Yazidi people Skip had met the year before. We arrived outside the camp, to a place called Grace Community Center, and we were immediately confronted by armed guards who checked our IDs, asked a few questions, and then let us go inside. This was the center we had donated money to.

It was a place for the people in the camp to eat and gather together. Out in front, the men learned carpentry and built their own tables or chairs or shelves. Inside, the women learned to cook healthy meals, but it also served as a separate place for them to process the things they had seen and been through. There they could talk quietly, privately, about the rape and abuse some of them had endured.

Down the hall there was a room to learn photography or sewing or art. The entire building was therapeutic and calm. It had been a brothel until Samaritan's Purse came in, cleaned it up, and opened it to refugees and IDPs. There was even a gynecological center to provide women with health care.

We got to see children playing on a playground. We went into the classroom and spoke with Aram, the second grader from Sinjar.

"First," he said, "the bad men came, and I ran to my grandmother's house. Then they came again, so we ran to my uncle's house. When the bad men came yet again, we found out they were called Daesh. Finally we came here, to Khanke Camp."

Hanging on the walls inside the building were paintings the children had made, therapeutic art meant to help them process the things they had seen. They were powerful pieces, provocative and piercing.

There was one painting we called "The Girl in Pink." The painting was a blonde-haired girl dressed in pink with a scar from her nose to her ear. Stitches held the wound together. Her shoulders were square, and she had little barrettes in her hair. Her face was blank, without expression.

The next one was a study in blue. The painting was of a blue tumultuous ocean that went up to a night sky holding a sad moon. The moon had a face with wrinkled eyes and a frown, and whatever it had seen was unspeakable. There was a hand coming up out of the water, like it was going down for the last time.

Just then an older woman dressed in a head covering and long robes approached me. She pointed at the blue moon painting and then to herself. She wanted me to know that her grandson had painted that troubling piece and that he was currently recovering from heart surgery. To me, the saddened moon and tumultuous waves expressed that nature itself grieved the violence against the Yazidis.

There was a third painting, a brown one, muddy, with two yellow hands coming up out of the muck. Above it was blue, the Yazidis venerated color, the color of royalty.

We went upstairs and met Marigold, a wonderful therapist to the children, and we even went into the room where she offered counseling. The entire Samaritan's Purse staff viewed this room as a holy place because here God did heart surgery—transforming hard hearts back to hearts of flesh as Ezekiel prophesied. We took off our shoes when we went inside to show our respect.

A door led out onto the roof of Grace Community Center, and from there we could see into the IDP camp itself, the acres of tents, stretched out as large as any city. I stood beside an American security guard who had come with us, and he started crying. When you see a guy built like Yul Brynner playing the Pharaoh in the movie *The Ten Commandments* shaken emotionally, you know the situation is dire.

"I could do this," he said quietly. "I could live here and help these people."

Our guides at the community center took me and a few other women in our group to sit down and talk with the Yazidi women. I was so eager to hear from the people who had played an important part in bringing me to Iraq. I still hoped to get to Mount Sinjar during this trip, but if I couldn't, at least I could hear from some Yazidi women in person.

We went out to our van and drove down the dusty road outside the camp. Even with tens of thousands of tents, I saw almost no people. They parked and we got out, walked through the wind. I tried walking closer to the tents, but I still didn't see anyone.

We came around a corner to where the buildings opened up, clearing space for a small gathering. I finally saw people, and our guide led us into a cinder block room. Several Yazidi women sat there, some with boys, but mostly older women. Marigold introduced us.

"Would you like to tell these American women your stories?" she asked them in her quiet voice.

They weren't shy.

"Why don't people know who the Yazidis are?" they asked us. "Why don't they know us? Why don't they care what is happening to us? Why isn't anyone helping?"

They were pleading with us, tears in their eyes. Some of them seemed almost angry.

"You must tell them!"

An older woman looked directly at me. "You are from America. Help us. Take us with you. Please."

I could feel their expectations, heavy and sincere. They had such intense needs, not only for themselves, but for their children, their husbands.

"I'm very small," I said to them. "I'm married to a pastor who speaks to many people, but I do not have power."

I paused.

"But I spoke with your leader a few days ago. We want to help. I spoke with Baba Chawish."

Their eyes lit up. I could hear them whispering to one another, "Baba Chawish, Baba Chawish, Baba Chawish."

"He said that we can come and help, and maybe we can build a playground here for you and your children. And my husband, he is a teacher. He is on the radio. I promise, when I get home, I will tell everyone I can about what is happening to you."

They were energized by our presence. I think they finally felt heard. I think they finally felt seen. They crowded in close to me, suddenly pulling out their cell phones.

"Did you know?" one of the women asked. "Did you hear that ISIS took a group of our girls, put them in a cage, paraded them down the streets of Mosul, and burned them alive?"

My stomach sank. Yes, I had heard that in the news just that morning.

"Yes," I said. "I was told that this happened."

"Watch," a few of them said at the same time, holding out their phones, video footage of the burning already playing on the small screens. It was terrible. But they wanted me to see it. They wanted me to watch it with them.

"I'm so sorry," I murmured. "I don't understand why people would do this to your people."

That video was probably the last thing on earth I wanted to see. Burning women, screaming in a cage in the middle of Mosul. But they needed me to see it. They needed me to experience it with them.

So I watched. I looked. And I didn't turn away.

Another seemingly random connection led us to a remote series of villages in the far northern reaches of Iraq. To get there, we drove on a highway that seemed to steadily go up and up and up. To the south and west stretched these incredible green plains. To the north were mountains ranges, each higher than the one before it.

After traveling for a few hours, we turned off of the highway and drove on a narrow road flanked by sheer cliffs on one side and a steep drop on the other. At the bottom of the chasm was a clear, rocky stream. We held on tight. The road passed by small groups of houses, small shops, soccer fields. Herds of goats and skinny cows brought us to a halt as they crossed or meandered along the road.

Finally, we crested one last peak, then descended an unpaved stone road into the Nahla Valley.

The Nahla Valley is located in the provinces of Nineveh and Dohuk and seems to be mostly populated by Kurdish Muslims and Assyrian

Christians. We were on our way to meet with a man named Yosef, a man who was interested in having us connect with, and build a playground for, his community.

I was amazed at what we learned.

Yosef was born in Kirkuk and lived in Baghdad for a time and then in Mosul. His grandfather was from this small village in Nahla, and he grew up visiting the valley on vacations.

"Many things happened in Mosul under ISIS," he said in a quiet voice. "These are things we do not talk about. These are things we will not explain. They are better left unsaid."

One day Yosef and his family left Mosul, away from his business and everything they owned, and took refuge in the Nahla Valley.

"Sometimes I miss Mosul," he said. "Yes, sometimes. But they destroyed everything, including our dreams. I was a civil engineer there, working with World Vision and other NGOs, but ISIS killed our manager. Of the 300 families I knew in Mosul, some were killed; others are now refugees around the world. Some moved to Turkey, Jordan, Lebanon, or Australia. Others have found villages like this one."

Their church in the Nahla Valley, built in 1925, was destroyed four times, most recently in 1993 under Saddam Hussein's soldiers.

He told us how refugees had fled into their village, running as far as they could from ISIS. These were refugees from Qaraqosh and Sinjar. The Nahla community, already living on the edge of poverty, had little to offer. But instead of encouraging or forcing the refugees to keep moving, they gave them what they had. They allowed the refugees to move into their church, into their homes, even into their businesses.

"Twenty-two families lived in our church for over a year. We have storefronts where we took everything out and let families live there. Over 300 IDP families have come through our village, and some are still here. I kept track of everyone, when they arrived, when they left."

The Christians in the Nahla Valley feel pressure from many sides. ISIS, though far away, has caused refugees to flee there. Their Muslim neighbors living in overpopulated villages are constantly trying to squat on their land. And the Turkish Air Force, which is in constant conflict with the PKK, will often bomb the surrounding mountains.

"The PKK, they hide in our valley," he said, shaking his head. "The Turkish planes come and bomb them. We were working on a project that would deliver more clean water to our village, and our workers wore orange vests so the bombers wouldn't mistake them for rebels, but then the PKK starting wearing the same clothing in order to blend in. It took us two extra months because our own workers had to flee from the bombers."

This village in the Nahla Valley is a beautiful, remote place. We got lost traveling there and were two and a half hours late. I love that it is so hard to get there yet God is there. To the people in Nahla Valley, our presence is the heavenly Father smiling down on them. To them, the aid we give is the answer to their prayers. When we help with water projects and playgrounds and soccer fields, something that seemed impossible becomes possible.

While we were visiting, we were informed some girls who had fled from Qaraqosh had prepared a dance for us. They came out in bright clothing, and though we could not understand the words to their song, there was deep grief and longing there that we did understand. Their arms waved slowly over their heads, and they bowed down low to the ground, remembering their wonderful city, their beautiful church, their close friends and family. It was a dance full of mourning and remembrance and hope.

I would think of their dance a year later when I walked through their defaced church, saw the bullets on the ground in the courtyard, and pulled a small wooden cross from the rubble. I would remember them when the priest told me he would teach the children about forgiveness.

After my trip to Khanke Camp and hearing the stories of the Yazidi people, my desire to physically stand on Mount Sinjar and help the Yazidis who were still there increased even more.

I spoke with Dave briefly that night. He knew how much I wanted to be on Sinjar, how long we had been praying against the black banners.

"We're in Mirky Village building one of your playgrounds," he told me on the phone. "I can sneak you up Mount Sinjar if you want."

It's hard to quantify danger levels when talking with Dave—the man has been in the middle of so many harrowing experiences that his danger meter isn't the same as everyone else's. I talked with our hosts for a long time about going up to Mount Sinjar. I so desperately wanted to go. But in the end, they decided it wasn't safe enough.

"I don't think we'll be able to make it up the mountain this time," I told Dave, explaining our hosts' concerns.

His offer was tempting. I knew he wanted us to be able to come, and he was even in the middle of building playgrounds for us on Mount Sinjar. I wanted so badly to see the Yazidi children playing and laughing on these new playgrounds! But in the end, in deference to our hosts, we declined.

We were so close. But it didn't happen. Not on that trip.

PART FIVE

On Top of Mount Sinjar

*"For the mountains shall depart
And the hills be removed,
But My kindness shall not depart from you,
Nor shall My covenant of peace be removed,"
Says the LORD.*

ISAIAH 54:10

12

A Trail of Sorrow

April 2017

We only have a few days left on our trip here in Iraq. I can't stop thinking about the things we have seen: the ISIS tunnels, the church, the hospital, the painted ISIS flag with the red writing over it that said, "Jesus is the light of the world." I keep hearing Murray, in all the different places where we have been, whispering, "Jesus, Jesus, Jesus." What a trip this has been. What an intense part of the world.

I speak with our hosts, still desperate to get to the top of Mount Sinjar. When the Yazidis fled up the mountain, when I saw the images of them starving, when I heard the stories of the massacre that had happened, it had been the beginning of my desire to come and help. Being on Mount Sinjar, seeing the playgrounds we have paid for and helped build, would bring things around full circle. I think of our trip there a year ago, when Dave offered to smuggle me up the mountain, when things weren't safe enough for us to go. Seeing what had happened in Sinjar had been such a huge catalyst for us to begin working in Iraq. I have wanted to walk on that mountain for three years. I have wanted to replace the black banners with our own banner proclaiming the words of Jesus, "Let the little children come to Me."

All week our hosts went back and forth: You can go, you can't go. You can go, you can't go. It's such an unpredictable area, the front lines of the war are so fluid, and unless you have people who can give you inside information on how the fight is going against ISIS, it's a tough call. Everything changes day by day. The distance from Sinjar city to ISIS can be measured in kilometers.

The host tells me we will give it a try tomorrow. Still no promises, but we will drive in that direction and see what happens. I go to bed eager and anxious for the morning.

It is morning now, and we load the team into the van, accepting the fact that the trip could be called off at any moment. ISIS is simply too close to make definite plans. We head in the direction of Sinjar province, and Murray plays his guitar quietly in the back. The sun is shining. It is a windy, clear day.

We settle into a long drive through wide, flat fields, but there are always mountains off in the distance, low and purple against the hazy sky. Summer is on the way. I wonder what the summer will bring for Kurdistan. For the rest of Iraq. I wonder what the summer will bring for the other places we've visited: Qaraqosh, Mosul, Erbil. We are close to the Syrian border now—looking through the windows on the passenger side of the van, I can see a large, manmade berm that runs parallel with the road.

"See that long pile of dirt?" our host asks us. "That's the Syrian border."

I think of the terror and pain the people on the other side of that long berm have experienced. I picture the little boy on the Greek beach, dead. I think of the little boy in the back of the ambulance, dumbstruck in the wake of another bombing. It seems the entire region could be summed up in that image: shocked, battered, emotionless after so much horror. I pray for Syria as our van continues toward Sinjar.

For one hour, and then two hours, we drive, and the landscape is empty of houses. The few we pass are abandoned or have been blown up. A few communities we pass are only half-built, construction halted when ISIS approached during the previous years. In front of us, the mountain draws closer, the color of dust. The road goes straight into it. Suddenly the road curves to the side, then doubles back. We are driving up Mount Sinjar.

There is a certain beauty to the side of the mountain—the low, handmade houses are built along deep gorges, and some rudimentary terracing has been done to create flat spaces for animals and crops. There is some green there, and I can tell those lush areas are not natural to the mountain, that the people who live there have fought hard for them. The road is winding, and always to the right there is a steep drop-off.

There is also an ancient feel to the place, as if we are driving back in time. There is nothing modern—no cars, no telephone poles, no paved grids. The people look strong, intense, weathered. The children walk over to the road and stare at our van as we drive past. The road is always climbing, climbing. It gets colder the higher we go.

We come to a checkpoint and slow down, but the guards wave us through without coming out of their hut. It seems that this area has returned to some kind of peace. I look back as we pass and realize they are Peshmerga fighters, and they are two women. They wear a scarf wrapped up over their head, and it also covers the bottom half of their face. Their eyes are piercing, and they carry automatic rifles slung over their shoulders, nonchalant, as if the weapons are backpacks or purses.

Even the women are responding to the call to fight.

I think of Deborah, the Old Testament hero who stepped in and led the Israelite army when no one else would. I love the spirit in women who are called to fight—I realize not all of us are, but I think I am. I think I am a Deborah. It seems strange to write this down, but it also feels true. I am, after all, Scottish. I am a scrapper. It's a realization I'm only beginning to unpack about myself, this willingness to go, to fight, to do. Following God into this adventure of leading Reload Love has taught me so much about myself.

We come around a corner, still climbing, and a wide mountain-top valley stretches out in front of us and to the right. The road curves slightly left, and we look out over a sea of white tents pitched in that valley. There are hundreds. Thousands? They are everywhere, and moving in between them are hundreds of people going about their daily routines. Many of them stop and watch as our van drives past.

These are the surviving Sinjar Yazidis, the ones who have not fled to other parts of the country, the ones who were not killed by ISIS, the ones who are waiting for Sinjar city to be cleared of landmines. These are the people I saw on the television three years before who were starving on top of the mountain. These people are the reason I am here.

This area where they live is windswept and cold and deserted. The ground is barren. And this is where they have lived, with very little protection from the summer's blistering heat or the winter's bone-chilling cold or the wind that never seems to let up. There is nowhere to run, nowhere to hide. Before the UN and Samaritan's Purse came with aid, there was no shelter.

I feel an overwhelming sense of despair driving through the makeshift IDP camp. It is a place that feels completely isolated from the world. These people feel alone and abandoned. Who will remember them? Who cares about this band of displaced Yazidis, camping on the top of this remote mountain? The Yazidis have known 70 genocides in their history, yet I get the feeling the persecution is not over for them. They are such a precious people, such a persevering people, seemingly nonviolent, only trying to live, eat, survive. They seem to be the people ISIS hate most—yes, the Christians, the Jews, and the Muslims who are not Muslim enough are also persecuted by ISIS, but the Yazidis are treated like animals.

I remember the woman wailing in the Yazidi temple. I remember sitting with Baba Chawish. I remember the black snake twisting its way up the side of the door.

We plan on stopping in the camp on our way back through. In the meantime, the road keeps climbing, even when I think it can't go any higher. There are no more trees, no more shrubs. We are approaching the top of the world. We drive along switchbacks, and the sea of tents fades behind us. At the curve of each switchback, I wonder if we have reached the top, but we keep climbing. It feels like we are very far from help if something goes wrong. It feels like some kind of frontier.

Finally, we reach the top. There is an outpost there, a clinic. There is a monument, a memorial that surrounds some kind of weapon that looks like a modern cannon. It is here that two brothers held off the advance of ISIS, kept them from coming over the mountain. There is an endless view down, down, down, all the way to Sinjar, sitting on the opposite side of the mountain we came up.

We begin our descent.

The road going down into Sinjar city is an endless series of tight switchbacks, each section of road maybe 50 to 100 yards long, curving into a steep turn downhill before moving on to another stretch. It is clear that we are entering a place that recently was a war zone. The road is covered with debris: clothing, furniture, vehicles that are broken down or blown up, only their blackened skeletons remaining. The other side of the mountain felt alive, ancient, untouched. This side feels violated. There are devastating untold stories all around me.

I look down into the gorges on both sides of the road and see cars that dropped hundreds of feet to the bottom. There is even an oil tanker there, the cab black and charred.

This is the side of the mountain people frantically climbed in order to escape ISIS, walking the heavy switchbacks in the heat of the day or the dark of night. They were traumatized people, victimized people. These were the old, the infirm, or the very young, lucky not to be dead or whored out by ISIS. These were the lucky ones?

Adrenaline gives us the ability to do superhuman things. I know that. I think about the fog of war that descends on a city at night, the chaos of trying to find family members, meet somewhere, get out of a city suddenly overrun by enemies. I think about the trauma of hearing guns going off, children screaming, adults wailing.

What can we do to give humanity back to the traumatized?

One of the women in the IDP camp we visited in 2016 told me about her family's escape from Sinjar when ISIS came on them suddenly. She had a sister who was unable to walk, so they tied ropes under her arms and dragged her up the mountain. I can't even imagine walking up that steep road, much less dragging someone by the armpits. Or being dragged.

Don't close your eyes. Keep looking. Let God tell you what to do.

I want to get out of the van and walk up that road, but we are short of time.

I imagine what it would be like trying to get up that mountain. Imagine the heat. The bullets firing over your head. The bombs and grenades going off in the city below you as you try to distance yourself from the chaos, the fighting. Imagine walking without any hope of food or shelter or water at the top.

Do you walk past the children who can go no farther?

Do you keep walking even when you see someone who is injured or wounded and needs medical attention?

Do you pass by the elderly man or woman who struggles to keep going?

Because if you stop, you will probably die. If you help someone, you will probably die.

How did they do it?

Our vans pass an empty sports stadium, weeds already growing up through the cement, and pause at the edge of Sinjar city. There is not another person in sight. There is not a sound except the wind blowing through the rubble. Every house and building is destroyed. Every street shows signs of wear.

"There is another ISIS tunnel here we can look at," our guide says, "but we have to stay out of the surrounding buildings. They haven't been cleared yet."

I can tell he's uncomfortable with the idea of us climbing around inside the rubble, and to be honest, I don't want to do it again. In this environment, in this place where there has recently been so much devastation and desolation, I just want to stand. I want to be, to take it in and bear witness that evil no longer controls that area.

On the edge of the city, along the side of the road, a square plot of ground has been roped off. Our van stops. We climb out, and the wind blows my hair around, kicks up the dust wherever I walk. Our group stands beside the roped off area, the high grass.

"That is a mass grave," our guide explains. "When ISIS came into the city, they rounded up a group of men and shot them when they wouldn't convert. We think there are 60 or 70 bodies here. The families are petitioning for DNA tests to be done so they can ID their loved ones."

I stare at the tall grass bending this way and that. I wonder if family members fled the city past the bodies of loved ones, lying in a pile. How could you leave, knowing your father, grandfather, uncle, or brother's body was lying there? How could you leave them behind?

It is a trail of sorrow, that road up the mountain.

That is a quiet, solemn moment, standing there under a sky blue and bright.

"Would you like to go see a few of your playgrounds?" our guide asks us.

I nod. I wipe tears from my eyes. We walk once around the mass grave. I can't help but wonder how many IEDs are hidden in the tall grass. We go back to the van, and leaving the bodies there feels improper. Simply standing and observing the place where they fell feels so insufficient. But again I am reminded of the ministry of presence. Sometimes the only thing we can do is stop and observe. Sometimes our tears are the only thing we have to offer.

We climb back into the van, and we take our silence with us. No one is talking as the van creeps along one of the main streets into Sinjar city. I can't help but think how long I've wanted to be here, how long I've wanted to see this place. And now, here I am, just a pastor's wife from Albuquerque, doing the next thing, taking the next step.

How did this happen? How did I, Lenya Heitzig, end up in a van driving through an abandoned city in Iraq?

We turn a corner and drive even deeper into the city. Crumbling buildings line both sides of the street. I don't see a single building untouched by war. In a place that once held around 75,000 people, I don't see a single soul.

The van pulls over. We climb out. I feel exposed there in the middle of that strange combination of chaos and silence. We walk down a side street, and there seems to be no one around. No one. We turn a corner, and in the middle of a field of weeds, I see it. I stop in my tracks.

It is one of our playgrounds.

The bright primary colors stand out against the surrounding destruction. The weeds are high around it, but in the midst of the playground, the ground is trampled flat. We wade through the high growth and stand beside the slide and swings. This is one of our smaller playgrounds, a simple structure that Dave Eubank's team put up for us when the front line was not far away.

As we stand there, a few children emerge from the surrounding neighborhoods. Where could they possibly be living? Which of these destroyed houses have they returned to? How do they know which houses are safe and which have been rigged with landmines or IEDs? The answer is, of course, that they do not know, and every day they play within reach of land mines, within arms' length of devices that could lead to disfigurement or dismemberment or death.

Tentatively, they approach us, smiling. One of them climbs the slide and goes down it, grinning. We give them a few small gifts we brought along in a Reload Love bag: an orange, a fruit drink, a good Samaritan coloring book with crayons.

More children start coming out as we return to our van, and we give them packs as well, say hello, ask how they are doing. I cannot believe there are families in this city. I cannot imagine where they get food, drinkable water. What do they do during the day, when the sun bakes down on their empty city? What do they do at night, when the cold settles in and mortars sound off in the distance or someone runs down their street? Do they listen for the approach of ISIS? Do they dream of what this city was like before the war?

We climb into the van, and again I do not know what to do with everything I am seeing. It is too much to process. We drive farther into the city, turn left, and park beside a building that used to be an ice cream business. Now it houses an NGO building doors and windows.

Across the street is another one of our playgrounds.

Jen and I wander around the grounds, swing on the swings, even take a trip down the slide. The installers of this playground put down some artificial turf, and it looks so nice. It's surrounded by a high, black chain-link fence, which I'm sure moms will someday appreciate when they can bring their prone-to-wandering children. The rest of the team walks the perimeter or sits on the benches. All around us are empty, destroyed buildings. Businesses with their gates smashed in. A ditch filled with rubble.

Sometimes people still ask me, "Why playgrounds? There are so many needs. Why not provide food or water or clothing first?" There are all the answers I've said before—the ministry of presence, the chance for mothers to get a break, the way playgrounds cannot contribute to a false economy—but now I have stood on playgrounds and watched traumatized children play and I know their worth.

Sinjar province now has seven playgrounds, both on the mountain and on either side of the city. It might not be a lot, but it's something, and on every playground is a banner that proclaims the name of Jesus. A banner that says, "Let the little children come to Me." On every playground, children are returning to some kind of normal life. On every playground, they are swinging or spinning or sliding, and every time they do, they forget, if only for an instant, the terror they have seen.

Professionals will tell you there are certain protocols you need to follow if you want to help a child recover from trauma. I've taken those and distilled them down into the acronym CAN. It doesn't matter if the child has experienced trauma at the hands of a gang in Chicago, a family member in New Mexico, or an ISIS terrorist in Iraq. These are the things that help them recover as quickly and effectively as possible.

The *C* stands for "Calm." The child needs to rediscover safety and security, which is why we partner with organizations to create these safe spaces. When kids have been taken out of harm's way, they need to feel safe. It could be a classroom, a music room, or a playground. When Aram told us on the playground at the Khanke IDP camp that he felt safe there, we knew we were giving him the opportunity to deescalate the terror he felt in his life.

The *A* stands for "Acknowledgment." This means giving children validation that what happened to them actually happened and to reinforce it was not their fault. They didn't create it. They aren't the bad guys. For example, Yazidi children need to understand that they do not deserve to be treated the way ISIS treated them.

Finally, the *N* stands for "Normalcy." I believe that if you can return children to a state of normalcy, their hearts will have a chance to heal, to return to something like the state they were in before they experienced terror. Maybe it's kicking a soccer ball. Maybe it's cooking a meal. Whatever it is, returning to some semblance of a normal life helps them imagine something better in their life, both now and in the future.

Can I tell you a story where I saw CAN work firsthand?

Recently my son was in a motorcycle accident, and his wife called me in a panic. I drove to the scene, praying the entire way, and when I arrived and saw his motorcycle, I nearly got out of my car and threw up. It was wedged under a car, shattered and broken.

When his wife arrived, their children were in the car with her. She was freaking out, and understandably so. The kids could see how affected she was, so they started losing it too. I realized I would have to be calm for the children.

Calm.

"Where's Nathan?" I asked her. "What's happened?"

"He's in the ambulance," she said, putting her kids in my backseat. The kids started wailing, "My daddy's broken!"

I told my daughter-in-law to do what she needed to do. I would take the kids. As she walked away, I turned to them.

"Let's pray," I said because I didn't know what else to do, but also because that is a way to acknowledge the problem. Talking to God. Asking Him to be with us.

Acknowledgment.

I started praying and they were still crying, but then my grandson said, "I have an idea. Mimi, we're going to pray and ask Jesus if Daddy is okay."

So he prayed.

"Oh, Jesus, help the doctors take care of Daddy and don't let Daddy be broken. Jesus, is Daddy okay?"

A short pause.

"Mimi, what does 'amen' mean?"

"It means you agree with the prayer."

"Okay, Mimi, say amen."

"Amen," I said.

He asked his sister three times if she agreed, and finally she said, "Amen" through her tears. I started singing "Jesus loves me," and Seth said he didn't hear Jesus yet, but we kept going,

We got to my house, and we did what we always did: We got in the hot tub and played. I was trying to reintroduce normal life into that chaotic, scary situation. My granddaughter floated in the water around me and melted like a noodle. I could sense her relaxing. Then I gave them a bath and we looked at a photo I have of Nathan when he was 12 years old. My granddaughter carried that photo around with her all night.

Normalcy.

We ate dinner together, and we held hands until they fell asleep.

Calm.

Acknowledgment.

Normalcy.

I saw my grandkids in trauma, and I know this process works. Playgrounds can help meet the need for these things in children. Swings are soothing, rocking children the way they were rocked as a baby. If you don't have your mother's arms or are missing a family member, a swing is marvelous. The thrill of a slide can help you forget your pain, if only for a moment. Chasing your friends around the playground can reintroduce normalcy into your life.

This is what I tell big donors when they approach me with skepticism about playgrounds. CAN is the way forward for these children. Playgrounds can be part of the answer.

We're trying to take back this territory from the horror and terror of the black banners of ISIS. We are trying to elevate love and forgiveness and healing. We are trying to help eliminate hate.

I swing on the swing, slowly drifting back and forth, and I feel like a little girl again. I look around and try to imagine this city alive again, people back in their homes, businesses thriving. I try to see the city through hopeful eyes. I imagine children playing on the swings, sliding down the slides. I imagine them seeing Jesus' name for the first time.

It's time to go, and we leave the city, passing by the businesses and houses and schools folded in on each other like a collapsed house of cards. There is the mass grave, the grass still bent. There is the stadium. We drive up the endless switchbacks, past the burned-out cars and clothes clinging to leafless, thorny bushes. We get to the top and begin the descent.

We stop at one of our playgrounds in the IDP camp, the sea of white tents, and the children come from every direction. They never stop coming, not while we sing songs, not while we tell the story of the good Samaritan, not while we hand out backpacks. Word radiates out through the camp, and they keep coming—50, 60, 70 children. They are still coming, even as we load the van, even as we hand out the last pack, even as we drive away. Eighty children. A hundred children. It is so hard to leave them. It is so hard to give them what feels like so little.

I look back through the square rear windows of the van. I see the playground, the children still running around it, still chasing each other. That is what we are leaving behind: hope, and the name of Jesus.

On the way back to our hotel, we stop at the Samaritan's Purse base in Sinjar province. It is on the opposite side of the mountain as Sinjar city. This town was once a dwelling place for ISIS. It feels like the lions' den. It is not as destroyed as the other cities and villages we have seen, but it feels very empty. We eat a delicious dinner with the team and our hosts. We sit and talk quietly about all we have seen. We are all emotionally drained.

There is a loud bang. I go on high alert.

"What was that?"

A few of the guys walk over to the closed gate and peer through the edges, down the street.

"Sounded like a firework to me," one man says.

Fireworks? I wonder. *Where do you get fireworks in Sinjar province?*

I am eating beside one of our hosts, and he chuckles to himself.

"What?" I ask.

"We've broken our three main rules for you today," he says.

"Really? And what are those?"

"Well, we drove a lot slower than we usually do," he says. "We stayed on the mountain longer than we usually do. And we never stay here after 3:00 p.m."

I look around the surrounding rooftops. I wonder if there are any people still loyal to ISIS living in this part of Sinjar. It seems like it would be so easy to hide in this sprawling town with narrow streets and dark alleys.

As we leave, our host points out a slogan spray-painted in black Arabic letters.

"What does it say?" I ask.

"This was one of ISIS's headquarters here in Sinjar. You can see the artwork over here: an ISIS flag and two palm trees. The writing says, 'Islam is a tree that is built on the backs of unbelievers. The tree is watered by blood.'"

The next morning as we eat breakfast, we hear that Turkey launched a missile attack against the PKK forces on top of Mount Sinjar the night before, destroying a checkpoint. This is a checkpoint we drove past only hours before the missiles hit. It is a reminder to me of the many different conflicts still going on here, some of which do not even involve ISIS, some of which will continue going on long after we leave unless forgiveness can find a place.

13

"Let Your Legacy Be Love"

April 2017

I didn't sleep well on the last night in our hotel here in Erbil, Kurdistan. The rooms are nice, and the beds are comfortable. The food is really good, and the dining room is up at the top of the building with 360-degree views of the city through glass windows that stretch nearly from the floor to the ceiling. But a heaviness has weighed down my heart. I kept waking up through the night, crying, praying, thinking about all I've seen.

I heard a story once about some Westerners who hired Sherpas to take them on a safari through the African jungle. After hiking long hours for many days, the guides stopped, sat down on the trail, and refused to move forward. The Westerners were, understandably, confused.

"C'mon!" they said. "We have to go! We have a schedule to keep!"

"No," one of the Sherpas said quietly. "We're waiting for our souls to catch up."

Here in Erbil, on the last day of our trip, I feel like I'm waiting for my soul to catch up.

There's a part of me that's bracing myself for reentry into the life that's waiting for me, the life of a well-to-do pastor's wife. I have a planned speaking engagement with a women's ministry in La Jolla, California, one of the most affluent places in the country, so it couldn't be more opposite from where I am right now and where I've been this week. In one week I'll have seen people who have nothing, and then I'll be in one of the wealthiest counties in the world.

Originally the women wanted me to talk about bravery, and I was going to teach on Joshua. I think more men and women in America need to soldier up! This is the Lord's army, the Lord's battle, and too many of us are not in it. Too many of us are on the sidelines. Too many of us are satisfied with low-hanging fruit.

So I thought I was heading there to tell them to soldier up, fight the good fight, run the race, and make a dent for the kingdom. Then I got a text while I was on this trip—they had changed their minds. They'd like me to talk about how precious they are.

Precious? Is that all we want, to be in a safe place and blow bubbles and color in coloring books? The American psyche can be so fragile. It's time for us to gear up and get ready.

I sometimes use the illustration of Joan of Arc, a simple peasant girl in the fields of France. She had a vision from God to go to the king and say, "If you fight this, you will win." The army didn't want to fight, but when she arrived with her message and told them that God had their back, they changed their minds. But that wasn't all—this peasant girl wanted to go into battle too. Her only request? Some used armor and any horse they could find.

I feel that way.

Just give me some used armor and a horse, and I'll ride into battle! I'll try to lift the morale of others! I'll show up where people think they need to be coddled and I'll motivate them to enter the fight.

I'll help people see the things they need to see.

I feel gratified and amazed and humbled by everything I've seen. Three years ago, I watched on TV as the Yazidis fled up Mount Sinjar, pursued by ISIS. I asked God in that moment, *How can we help these people?* I wanted to be there to give them water, to do something, anything!

By the grace of God, we did it. We built a playground on the top of that mountain. I looked out over Sinjar city, out over the handful of people who are still living there, and I was humbled. How many people see something, pray that they can somehow make a difference, and then get to experience what I've been able to experience?

I feel so small. Only God could make this happen.

But as I sit here in this hotel, there's still a deep sadness. I still haven't processed that my feet walked where ISIS feet walked. I still haven't processed all the horror they've wreaked on this region. I haven't processed the children and parents I met in the hospital and the lives they have lived. I was completely taken aback by the church in Qaraqosh, the church that was burned and its courtyard used as a firing range. I haven't processed the image of the priest and the nun searching the rubble for the missing part of their flannel board.

I hold the small wooden cross in my hand, the one the priest let me take, and I pray for that church, that city. I pray forgiveness would sweep through the region like that constant wind.

It will take time to absorb what I have seen.

I'm so proud of our team. They were magnificent. There wasn't a weak link, not a weak moment. We were completely united throughout the trip. We took turns leading devotions each morning, and every single one was a word straight from God that spoke to us. I feel like they were the spiritual special forces, the precise people we needed to accomplish the tasks we were sent to do. God sent each of us here for a reason, and our roles became clearer as the trip went on. There was no division. Only unity and purpose and dedication.

I've learned a lot on this trip about the power of presence. You know, Reload Love is growing, but we are still a small organization with limited resources. Yet we do what we can with what we have. Still, the needs are so great.

At first I wondered, *What difference did we make?*

But the people here know someone cares enough to come all that way. And they were able to feed us and give us coffee and tea, show us hospitality, all of which makes them feel like they have something to offer too.

"We have been witnesses," one of the men said to us. "We've witnessed Saddam come and go. We've seen ISIS and the PKK and Turkey dropping bombs on our mountainsides. We have seen a lot." These are people in small villages with no stake in the geopolitical earthquakes. But we sat with them, and they were able to tell us what they've seen. Our simple presence helped validate their experience.

How can we know God's will when we're confronted with so many needs, so many people in misery, and so much evil?

I think of Abraham in his old age, looking for a wife for his son Isaac. Remember how he sent his oldest servant, the one in charge of everything he owned, to find a woman for him?

> So Abraham said to the oldest servant of his house, who ruled over all that he had, "Please, put your hand under my thigh, and I will make you swear by the LORD, the God of heaven and the God of the earth, that you will not take a wife for my son from the daughters of the Canaanites, among whom I dwell; but you shall go to my country and to my family, and take a wife for my son Isaac" (Genesis 24:2-4).

What a huge responsibility Abraham gave him! What an awesome task, to find the woman who would marry this long-desired son and continue the family lineage for God's chosen people!

So the servant went to the land of Abraham's ancestors, and once he was there he found himself at a well. How would he know who should marry Isaac, his master's son?

> Then he said, "O LORD God of my master Abraham, please give me success this day, and show kindness to my master Abraham. Behold, here I stand by the well of water, and the daughters of the men of the city are coming out to draw water. Now let it be that the young woman to whom I say, 'Please let down your pitcher that I may drink,' and she says, 'Drink, and I will also give your camels a drink'—let her be the one You have appointed for Your servant Isaac. And by this I will know that You have shown kindness to my master" (Genesis 24:12-14).

That's when Rebekah arrived, and he asked if she could give him a drink. She did, but she offered to water his camels as well, and the servant of Abraham knew this was the woman who was called to be Isaac's wife.

This is when the servant of Abraham said something that I think informs all of us how to find the will of God. He said, "Blessed be the LORD God of my master Abraham, who has not forsaken His mercy and His truth toward my master. As for me, being on the way, the LORD led me to the house of my master's brethren" (Genesis 24:27).

Did you see that? The servant said, "As for me, being on the way…" That's it! That's one of the best ways we can decipher God's will for us and discover our calling—be on the way! It's so much easier to guide a rolling stone than to get a boulder out of the hollow it has created in the ground.

So I keep moving. I keep asking God questions.

Are You leading Reload Love to Qaraqosh?

Are You leading us back to Sinjar?

Are You leading us to somewhere entirely new, to undiscovered, high-hanging fruit that no one else is reaching for?

It's easier for me to see God's will when I'm moving than when I'm at home, sitting on the couch. It's easier to hear answers when I'm asking questions.

I turned 60 years old in 2017. In ten years, I'll be 70. I'm not huge on making five- and ten-year plans. I tend to try to stay in the moment and follow where God is leading me today, but recently someone asked me what I'd like to see in Reload Love ten years from now. The question caught me off guard. I stopped for a moment and felt tears rising.

My best response to this question comes out of a story that happened on this trip.

We were at the hospital in Mosul, and Murray was playing his guitar for the children inside the pediatric area, in the tent for boys. The Reload Love team members were talking to different people, having their own encounters, and at that point I was sort of standing back and observing. That's when I saw a father without a child. He had that weathered, Middle Eastern look, with dark hair and dark eyes and a few days' stubble on his cheeks. A large moustache hid his upper lip. His shoulders were slumped—I could tell he was at the end of his rope.

I asked the translator to talk to him, and she was able to find out that this man's son was in surgery. He stood there, observing everything, but as Murray was singing we made eye contact, this man and I, and I think our gazes meeting was perhaps more emotional than he expected. He started to tear up, and he turned away so as not to cry in front of me. He sat down on what I am assuming was his son's empty cot, and he leaned forward. He reached up and covered his face with one of his hands.

I know in that culture it's not acceptable, but I had an overwhelming urge to walk over and put my hands on his shoulders as a sign of friendship, as a tangible gift of my presence. So I did. I walked about ten feet to where he sat, and I stood behind him, and I put my very white, very Western hands on his shoulders.

He was weighed down by the world. And he started sobbing. Heaving. He was covering his face with both hands then, gasping for air. I know something of that feeling, having been with many suffering people. I know that when we as human beings experience anxiety, it can be a weightless feeling, as if we're floating away without an anchor. Or as if we might explode. It can be terrifying.

At home in Albuquerque, when our dogs freak out, we have these things called thunder vests, which are basically weighted jackets, and when we wrap those tightly around them, it helps them feel grounded and safe. I wonder if it isn't the same for us human beings. I put my hands on the man's shoulders to weigh him down, to help him feel less like he might float away.

As I stood there, the Lord told me to pray Psalm 23 over him:

> The LORD is my shepherd;
> I shall not want.
> He makes me to lie down in green pastures;
> He leads me beside the still waters.
> He restores my soul;
> He leads me in the paths of righteousness
> For His name's sake.

Yea, though I walk through the valley of the shadow of death,
I will fear no evil;
For You are with me;
Your rod and Your staff, they comfort me.

You prepare a table before me in the presence of my enemies;
You anoint my head with oil;
My cup runs over.
Surely goodness and mercy shall follow me
All the days of my life;
And I will dwell in the house of the LORD
Forever.

I felt myself stopping for a long time at "restore his soul." I kept praying that, repeating it. And then, again, when I came to "goodness and mercy shall follow him," I felt myself pause there and pray those words over this Iraqi man, over and over again.

Restore his soul.

Goodness and mercy.

The interpreter had followed me over, and I wondered if he would ask if the man was okay. The interpreter and the man had a brief conversation, back and forth, and then he turned to me.

"He says his emotions have come because of the fact that his own people are killing each other. Brothers are killing brothers. They are filled with so much hate and so much revenge that they hurt each other, and it feels like an endless cycle."

The interpreter paused, then continued. "He says, yet here you are, showing them love. It is hard for him to comprehend why you Americans would come all this way to show him love when his own people have shown each other so much hate."

Can we do anything more than that? As believers, as Christians, as followers of Christ, isn't that our highest calling? The interpreter cleared his throat and said one more thing.

"This man also says his heart is empty of all happiness."

I nodded.

"When I prayed for him," I replied, "I prayed Psalm 23 from our

Bible, and it's about our God who is a good Shepherd. He will come to you and restore your soul. I believe God can make your heart new."

The interpreter conveyed this to the man, and he nodded politely and wiped his eyes.

"*Inch'Allah*," he said, which means "God willing," but can also be used to voice skepticism, sort of the way Abraham responded to the news that he would have a son in his old age. "Sure, God willing!"

"I wish our country would have more mercy," the man said.

I smiled. "At the end of that psalm, it says that if you follow the Shepherd, mercy will follow you. Goodness and mercy. If you follow Him, He'll restore your heart."

"*Inch'Allah*," he said again, but I like to think there was hope in his voice this time, perhaps the smallest belief that goodness and mercy could return to him, to his country, to his people.

What dreams do I have for Reload Love in the next ten years?

I remember chatting with a friend during one of our brainstorming sessions. One day, after we had been building playgrounds in the Middle East for quite some time, he asked me a question. "Have you heard of the Silk Road?"

"You mean like Marco Polo? That Silk Road?"

He nodded.

"Of course I've heard of it," I said.

"There are ancient way stations that stretch all along the Silk Road. Back in those days, all communication, all trade, all culture, even the development of languages, took place along the Silk Road. People still live along the Silk Road, they still travel along the Silk Road, and if you invest in one of those communities, everyone finds out about it. They don't really care about the Internet or social media as much as we do; everything is verbal. Everything is tribal."

I love that word. It made my ears perk up.

"The Silk Road basically goes all the way from China, through the Middle East, and right up to Israel. According to the Bible, that's where things will end. Right there. And you are already building playgrounds in one section of it. What if you continued building playgrounds along the ancient Silk Road?" he asked, and I could tell the idea excited him.

"What if this is how you approached your mission? Because if you invested in these communities, if you put up banners on these playgrounds that said, 'Let the little children come to Me—Jesus,' the word would spread far and wide."

That image solidified in my mind.

"If you really want to go to the uttermost parts of the world," he continued, "what about the Silk Road? Why not go there?"

Who knows where God will lead us in the coming years?

All I know is this: I hope that every single person we encounter sees the mercy of God, the love of God. I hope every interaction we have is one small step in reversing the cycle of violence begetting more violence. I hope that Reload Love becomes a vehicle that helps de-radicalize the world, that pushes the tide in the other direction. I hope every child who plays on our playgrounds becomes part of a generation who learns forgiveness, love, mercy, and peace at an early age.

Let the little children come to Me.

As Jen is always saying, "Let your legacy be love."

What began with only 12 disciples has spread love through the world. It was a grassroots effort that started in Jerusalem and has gone to the ends of the earth. What we're trying to do can only be spread from heart to heart.

That's the new dream that I have.

That's what I'd like to see.

Afterword

Dave Eubank and his beautiful family came to visit our church in Albuquerque in the summer of 2017, only a few months after I had crawled through ISIS tunnels and seen the X-ray of the bullet next to the girl's heart and stood on Mount Sinjar. They came to share their story with our church, to rally our people behind their mission and the mission of Reload Love. Our paths have become so inextricably entwined. It continues to amaze me that, of all the people in the world, God would lead me to Dave Eubank, deep in the jungles of Burma, and that we would both go to Iraq to help children.

Our teams met up for breakfast on Monday morning, the day Dave and his family were planning on heading out. We took up a large table in their hotel's restaurant, and we talked about all the things we had seen. We talked about what God was doing. We dreamed about where we might go next: Syria? Africa? Back to Burma? I thought about the last time we dreamed together, when God led us from Burma to Iraq.

Who knows where the next open door might lead us?

As we sat there, Dave got one of his signature, slightly mischievous smiles on his face.

"I brought a gift back for you, Lenya," he said in a loud, matter-of-fact voice.

"You did?" I asked. "That's kind of you!"

"Yeah," he said. "Let me go get it for you. You're going to love this."

He went out to his truck and came back in carrying some kind of shopping bag. He reached inside and pulled out something I never expected to see in Albuquerque. In fact, I never expected to see this thing so close up, no matter where I might be in the world.

Dave Eubank handed me an ISIS flag.

When I took it from him, I felt like I was accepting a live snake.

"I got that in Mosul," he said, grinning. "The Iraqi forces moved forward and took over an area ISIS had controlled. Their flag was still flying, way up at the top of a 30-foot flagpole. No one wanted to climb up to get it because they thought they might get shot, but I didn't know if I'd ever have another chance to snag one of these things. So I climbed up and brought it down."

"Dave!" I said. "That's crazy."

"I know," he said, smiling again. "But as soon as I got down, everyone wanted it. You wouldn't believe how much money some of those soldiers offered me for this flag."

He laughed, then quieted down. Suddenly his voice was filled with kindness and appreciation.

"I knew you would appreciate it."

We unfolded it, and I stared at the white writing on the black cloth. The white script at the top reads, "There is no god but Allah. Mohammad is the messenger of Allah." Beneath it, in a white circle with black writing, are Arabic words that say, "Mohammad is the messenger of God." It's meant to resemble the Prophet's seal.[5] ISIS used the flag because they hoped it would be a unifying force that would reach out to all Muslim people and not just the ones who had already joined their cause.

"Because the ISIS flag has the name of Allah on it, some of their Muslim enemies were hesitant to shoot in its direction, afraid they might shoot the name of Allah," Dave told us.

It lay there on the table, and all of us stared at it. There was something sinister about the flag, especially when I thought about all the atrocities it had looked down on: the torture and the rape and the persecution of so many innocent people. The destruction of entire cities. The hate for entire groups of people it spread. Pure evil took place under the watchful gaze of this ISIS symbol. Part of me wanted to burn it and to revel in its destruction.

But there was also something powerful about the imagery of me possessing it. There I was, a woman, a Christian, now in possession of their flag. I thought about how we prayed against this black banner, literally for years. I thought about how, in the midst of that migraine, I had realized what we were up against: no longer the Iron Curtain or the Bamboo Curtain but the Black Curtain of ISIS. I thought about how we had wanted to replace these black banners with banners that proclaimed the name of Jesus, and I pictured the playgrounds spread out across the Middle East that now had those banners flying over them.

I felt tears rising.

What other proof do we need that God will guide our steps? He took a regular woman like me from the heart of Albuquerque, New Mexico. I told Him I wanted to help children impacted by terror, and in the end, God led our team not only to provide relief supplies and education for displaced children but to build playgrounds that are helping children heal.

And as some incredible gesture, God handed me an ISIS flag.

I have to admit, it felt like the biggest confirmation, as well as an encouragement to continue on.

Notes

1. Eve Ensler, "Yazidi Activist Nadia Murad Speaks Out on the 'Holocaust' of Her People in Iraq," *Time*, August 3, 2016, http://time.com/4435297/sinjar-anniversary-yazidi-nadia-murad/.

2. "The Legend of the Lost Book of Gold," *Wheat and Tares*, October 4, 2011, https://wheatandtares.org/2011/10/04/the-legend-of-the-lost-book-of-gold-part-1-of-4/.

3. "Greg Birch," June 29, 2016, https://www.americantriggerpullers.com/blogs/badass-trigger-pullers/greg-birch.

4. Ali Soufan, *The Black Banners* (New York: W.W. Norton & Company, 2011), xvii.

5. Kashmira Gander, "ISIS Flag: What Do the Words Mean and What Are Its Origins," *Independent*, July 6, 2015, http://www.independent.co.uk/news/world/middle-east/isis-flag-what-do-the-words-mean-and-what-are-its-origins-10369601.html

About the Author

Lenya Heitzig is an award-winning author and speaker whose passion for women, God's Word, and worship helps others recognize God's miraculous hand in the midst of the mundane. As the executive director of *she* Ministries and Reload Love at Calvary Albuquerque, Lenya encourages thousands of women each year to see God's Word do His work in their lives through weekly Bible studies, national conferences, and regional retreats. Lenya's heart is to reach out to hurting people through tangible acts of love. After September 11, 2001, she launched Mercy B.A.N.D.s (Bearing Another's Name Daily), silver bracelets inscribed with the names of individual casualties of terror. Over 60,000 people, including 2,000 family members directly impacted by 9/11, have worn these poignant bands. Lenya also launched Reload Love, which touches the lives of those affected by terrorism.

RELOAD LOVE

READY. AIM. FREE.

There are three key elements in recovering from trauma: safety, acknowledgement, and normalcy. Reload Love helps to meet these needs in a variety of ways—sending food, medical aid, and relief supplies. We have found that one of the most impactful and long-lasting ways to help is building playgrounds. Playgrounds restore a sense of normalcy by creating a safe space for children to laugh, play, and let everything go.

We raise awareness by transforming spent bullet casings into beautiful brass jewelry. When you wear a piece, you help us raise awareness and advocate for children around the world who have been caught in the crossfire of terrorism.

If you would like to donate or
subscribe to our blog, please visit

RELOADLOVE.COM